PLANETARY

STRENGTH

A Commentary on Morinus

Bob Makransky

THE WESSEX ASTROLOGER

Published in 2010 by
The Wessex Astrologer Ltd
4A Woodside Road
Bournemouth
BH5 2AZ
England

www.wessexastrologer.com

ISBN 9781902405506

A catalogue record of this book is available at The British Library

Cover design by Dave at Creative Byte, Poole, Dorset

Astrological charts calculated using Solar Fire Gold

Contents

Glossary   i

Introduction   v

Chapter 1: Celestial State   1

Chapter 2: Terrestrial State   18

Chapter 3: Aspectual State   41

Chapter 4: Comparison of Different Canons of
            Planetary Strength   64

Chapter 5: Other Dignities   80

Appendix 1: The Local Determination   103

Appendix 2: Dr. Jones' Methodology   117

Natal Horoscope of Jean Baptiste Morin de Villefranche   122

Index   123

Jean Baptiste Morin de Villefranche (1583 - 1656)

Glossary

Celestial state = *Essential Dignity* = dignity or debility due to position in the zodiac of signs. Considered to be good if a planet is in its ruling or exaltation sign (Morinus would include its triplicity here also) and considered to be bad if *essentially debilitated* in its detriment or fall. A planet's ruling sign is also known as its *Domicile*, and its sign of detriment is also known as its *Exile*. If a planet is in a sign in which it is neither in good nor bad celestial state, then it is said to be *Peregrine*. For planets which have two ruling signs, "that one of its domiciles is called its *joy* which corresponds more closely to its ruler, either by reason of its principal nature, or by reason of its sex, or by reason of its more tempered effect or influx." [Morinus Book 15, chapter 12. Holden page 236]. Thus the joy of Saturn is Capricorn; of Jupiter Sagittarius; of Mars Aries; of Venus Libra; and of Mercury Virgo.

Triplicity = an essential dignity used by Morinus of lesser strength than ruler or exaltation. There are different schemes of *triplicities* in existence. The one which Morinus advocates gives the dignity of *triplicity* to planets when they are in the following signs: Sun, Mars, and Jupiter in fire signs; Mercury, Saturn, and Venus in earth signs; Saturn, Venus, and Mercury in air signs; Jupiter, Moon, and Mars in water signs.

Terms = an essential dignity of uneven divisions of each sign ruled by the seven classical planets. This dignity is not used by Morinus, but two different systems of allocating terms and their rulerships are mentioned by Ptolemy [*Tetrabiblos I*, 20-21]. Morinus specifically rejects certain other traditional essential dignities and attributions of qualities to zodiacal degrees such as "the novenas, the bright degrees, the smoky degrees, the monomoiriai, etc. which are nothing other than mere symbols of the ineptitude, stupidity, and insanity of men who were ignorant of the principles of this divine science, which follies the wiser astrologers have always disdained." [Morinus Book 15, chapter 13. Holden page 238].

The *dispositor* of a given planet is that planet which rules the sign in which the given planet is located. For example, since Jupiter rules Sagittarius and Pisces, then it is said to be the *dispositor* of any planets located in Sagittarius or Pisces. It can happen that all of the planets, by a series of removes in *disposition*, work back to one planet – termed the *sole dispositor* – which is in its own ruling sign. As an example, in Charlie Chaplin's chart Venus is the *sole dispositor* since Venus is in its ruling sign, Taurus; Venus disposes of Sun and Mars posited in Taurus; Sun and Mars in turn dispose of Saturn in Leo and Mercury in Aries, respectively; finally Saturn disposes of Moon and Jupiter in Capricorn.

When two planets each occupy a sign ruled by, or in the exaltation sign of, the other, then they are said to be in *mutual reception*. There is one possibility of a grand trine in reception, which happens when the Moon is in Pisces, Venus is in Cancer, and Jupiter is in Taurus.

Accidental dignities include: *terrestrial state* (angular/cadent); *aspectual state* (unaspected/well-aspected/afflicted); conjunct a bright *fixed star*, and *stationary* in motion. *Accidental debilities* include being cadent and afflicted.

Terrestrial state = dignity or debility due to house position (angular, succedent, or cadent). The angular houses are the 1st, 4th, 7th, and 10th; succedent houses are the 2nd, 5th, 8th, and 11th; cadent houses are the 3rd, 6th, 9th, and 12th.

Configurations, or *structures*, are complex aspects (of three or more planets) such as: grand trines, T-crosses, fans, wedges, grand squares, kites, rectangles, trapezoids, etc.

Synodic Phase (Oriental/Occidental) = a planet is *oriental* if it rises before the Sun in the east (within 180° of longitude before the Sun's longitude), and it is *occidental* if it sets after the Sun in the west (within 180° of longitude after the Sun's longitude).

Applying/separating = in Morinus' nomenclature a swifter planet applies to a slower one. However, it would seem more logical to define an applying aspect as one in which the orb of inexactitude is decreasing, and a separating aspect as one in which the orb of inexactitude is increasing. "One should also note whether a planet's aspect is applying or separating, since – all other things being equal – application has greater effect than separation." [Morinus Book 21, page 82].

Dexter/sinister = a dexter sextile, square, or trine is one in which the swifter planet is moving from conjunction to opposition with the slower planet, and a sinister aspect is one in which the swifter planet is moving from opposition to conjunction with the slower planet (in the case of the Moon and Sun, dexter = waxing and sinister = waning). "The sinister aspects (between the planets) will generally be stronger than the dexter." [Morinus Book 21, page 85].

Introduction

I recently read the excellent new Pepita Sanchez Llacer /Anthony LaBruzza translation of Morinus' (Jean Baptiste Morin de Villefranche, 1583-1656) *Astrologia Gallica Book XVIII*[1] – hereinafter referred to as Morinus Book 18 – and it got me to thinking about what exactly astrologers mean by the term 'strength'.

After all, the utter arbitrariness of the sign rulerships and exaltations is shown by the fact that users of both the tropical and sidereal zodiacs embrace the same system of essential dignities – even though, at the present time, they are shifted by one sign. So when for example Venus is in its ruler (Taurus) in the tropical zodiac, it is in its detriment (Aries) in the sidereal zodiac (the indications reverse for Libra – Scorpio and of course for Mars), and the exaltations of Venus and Jupiter (Pisces and Cancer respectively) mix up with their detriments (Aries and Gemini) between the two zodiacs as well. And yet both tropical and sidereal astrologers claim to find their respective systems of essential dignities valid. So, evidently they are looking at different things –

---

1. *Astrologia Gallica Book Eighteen* by J. B. Morin, translated by Pepita Sanchis Llacer and Anthony LaBruzza, AFA 2004, (ISBN-10: 0866905545; ISBN-13: 978-0866905541), is available at: http://www.amazon.com/Astrologia-Gallica-Book-Eighteen-Morin/ dp/0866905545/ref=sr_1_1?ie=UTF8&s=books&qid=1205437096&s r=8-1. It is strongly recommended that anyone who aspires to master the art of horoscope interpretation purchase and study this book thoroughly; as well as Morinus' *Astrologia Gallica Book XXI* (referred to in this book as Morinus Book 21), available in translation by Richard S. Baldwin as *The Morinus System of Horoscope Interpretation*, AFA 1974; and also by Lucy Little with a commentary as *Astrosynthesis*, Zoltan Mason 1974. Quotations cited as Morinus Book 21 refer to the Baldwin edition. See also *Astrologia Gallica Book Twenty-Two – Directions*, translated by James Herschel Holden, AFA 1994 ISBN-10: 0866904255. This book deals principally with Regiomontanus primary directions, but its appendices include selections from other books of *Astrologia Gallica*; quotations from this source are referred to in this book as *Morinus Book – Holden*.

defining 'strength' differently. (As we shall see later on when considering retrogradation as a strength factor, the Vedic astrologers do indeed have very different thoughts on what constitutes 'strength' than we occidentals do). Which leads us back to the central question, "What do we mean by 'strength'?"

The term 'strength' is bandied about rather loosely in astrology. It will be the purpose of this book to take a look at some different kinds of 'strengths' as they are explained in Morinus Book 18, and to examine what these imply in terms of corresponding character traits in the interpretation of natal horoscopes. You will derive the most benefit from this book if you have been studying astrology for at least a year and you have read and digested some basic books on horoscope interpretation. It is also assumed that you have collected at least several dozen example horoscope charts of people you know well, and that you understand the rudiments of what the different planets, signs, and houses symbolize.

Morinus defines strength as follows: "The strength of a planet can be differentiated from its virtue in that virtue, properly speaking, refers to a planet's essential or influential nature, by means of which the planet itself acts, whereas strength refers to the quantity of such virtue. Consider, for example, two magnets of equal size, one of which can lift 2 pounds and the other 12 pounds. They are clearly identical in virtue, that is, the ability to attract iron. But the two magnets differ in force or strength, because they have different quantities of such virtue. Therefore the strength of a planet seems correctly to be defined if one says that the strength of a planet is the quantity of virtue with which the planet itself acts." [Morinus Book 18, page 6].

Moreover, Morinus points out that some planets are intrinsically stronger than others: "Planetary strength, however, may be of two types: intrinsic strength and extrinsic strength. Intrinsic strength is a measure of the quantity of intrinsic virtue by which a given planet acts, in and of itself. (The ancient texts spoke of intrinsic strength generally ... when they said that the Sun and the Moon were more powerful than the other planets, and that the superior planets were [in general] more powerful than the inferior ones). On the other hand, extrinsic strength is a measure of the power (strength) of a planet determined by extrinsic factors, such as the planet's celestial state in the heavens, its position with respect to the horizon, and so on." [Morinus Book 18, page 6].

While the foregoing definitions are valid and useful, we must keep in the mind the human element in horoscope interpretation. Horoscopes are interpreted by people (computers could never do this, no matter how many rules you program into them, since all 'rules' of horoscope interpretation are merely rules of thumb). Just as quantum physics tells us that the state of a system is influenced by anyone observing that system, so too is horoscope interpretation influenced by the astrologer doing the interpreting.

A Vedic astrologer may consider of enormous importance factors which occidental astrologers ignore completely; and vice versa. There's no contradiction in this. A classroom of art students painting the same subject will come up with a great variety of interpretations of what they see. This doesn't make one right and another wrong; although obviously some artists are 'better' than others – their interpretations are deeper or more 'right on'.

The answer to the question, "What are we talking about?" is that we are talking about ourselves; i.e. science is not so much a description of the universe as it is a description of human perception of the universe. All we can ever describe is our own system of prejudices, since anything that is going on out there beyond the compass of our prejudices is by definition, indescribable. This is not such an abstract idea: we all know that to feel a feeling is not the same thing as to talk about it – a feeling cannot be captured in words, except for poetry. Neither can the universe be described in words, nor by any rational process (except, perhaps, by poetry).

Similarly, trying to express in words what a given astrological signature means in human life is impossible, because it can only be a feeling, and that feeling will be different for every astrologer, depending on your individual experience and interest in the field and in human nature. Therefore, books on astrological interpretation can succeed only to the extent that they succeed as poetry (as W.B. Yeats did in *A Vision*).

One way in which we might define 'strength' is *increased capacity for free choice*. Where the Vedic system contradicts the occidental system it is perhaps because Hindus regard 'strength' to be the capacity to *accept* one's karma and destiny rather than to *control* them; i.e. they thus would take an opposing view of what strength is all about (this is but a speculation – not something I feel like defending). A planet may be strong because it is in its ruling sign, angular, high in Astrodynes (in the Church of Light's methodology) etc., or in the Vedic system because it is high in Shad Bala.[2] All of these methods of assigning strength are different ways of assigning importance to one type or another of capacity to act with free choice, and debility in this context refers to bondage or inability to exercise free choice. Strong planets show where and how in a person's life they can realize their own desires and control their own destiny. They are productive of ease, tranquility, contentment. By contrast, weak planets show a helplessness or vulnerability – a cringing or defensiveness. Strong planets are good for material things and weak planets are good for spiritual things, such as learning self-denial (which may be the root of the contradictions encountered between the Vedic and occidental definitions of strength).

Like the Vedic and Church of Light methods, Morinus Book 18 propounds a system of scoring points based upon different strength factors, to arrive at overall totals for each planet. However, while it is quite tempting to try to concoct a scheme of counting points to determine which planets are strongest (most effective), and this analysis can indeed be valid, it is our purpose here to distinguish between different kinds of strength, rather than to subsume them all under a pseudo-mathematical calculation. It *is* important to determine which planet or planets are the most powerful for good or evil, and which are the least powerful, because in judging progressions and transits, and when making elections, a planet which is weak in the natal chart will produce little good subsequently. However, a planet which is strong in the natal chart will produce good, even through its nominally disharmonious aspects.

This is the alpha and omega in all predictive and electional work (choosing propitious times to begin various activities, and propitious places for various purposes). For example, in astrolocality work – to determine favorable/unfavorable places to live or to visit by projecting the natal horoscope onto a world map and observing where on the earth the planetary aspect lines lie – it is important to work with your strongest planets. A weak, afflicted natal planet will never bring fulfillment into your life even if it is nominally a benefic. As an example, on an

---

2. Shad Bala and Astrodynes are measures of planetary strength in the Vedic and Church of Light systems, respectively.

astrolocality map, if Saturn is strong in the natal chart, then even places on earth which are square Saturn (which lie on a square Saturn power line) will prove ultimately favorable (although they will certainly be places of struggle or increased responsibility). On the other hand, if Venus is natally weak then even the places on Venus' trine and sextile lines will be places of ultimate disillusion or disappointment of expectations; difficulties with women etc. This is what we find in predictive work as well: if planet X afflicts planet Y in the natal chart, then their subsequent trine or sextile will be disappointing (at best) rather than happy – the progression or transit will bring out the underlying affliction; if they are natally sextile or trine, then a subsequent progressed or transiting square will be ultimately beneficial (even if it is initially disruptive).[3]

Just as contradictory testimonies don't contradict in the person's personality (but are exhibited at different times), so too do testimonies of similar personality traits (for example of dominance, cooperativeness, absolutism, timidity, dourness, humor, whatever) tend to 'add up', to reinforce each other. Lots of testimonies to a positive, lucky attitude tend to make that the person's thought form predilection, and lots of testimonies to anger and vindictiveness tend to make *that* the person's usual thought form state.

In the present analysis, the principle criteria for determining strength are (in order of descending importance):

> Unaspected (forms no 6° Ptolemaic aspect)
> Conjunct an angle
> Stationary
> Sole dispositor
> Well-aspected
> In ruling sign / exaltation
> Conjunct a bright benefic fixed star

---

3. Remember this simple rule of thumb for interpreting transits, progressions, and directions: the moving body symbolizes the type of outer event or experience to be expected, and the planet or point contacted in the natal horoscope symbolizes your inner (emotional) response to this event. Therefore, if you have well-aspected natal planets, then fortunate events tend to happen to you in life; if afflicted, then the reverse.

(Note that the foregoing list is my personal opinion and differs from Morinus' view; he would consider the principle factors to be, in order: ruling sign/exaltation; angular; well-aspected).

Since a planet can be in bad celestial state (detriment or fall) yet still be in good terrestrial state (conjunct an angle), then obviously the various types of strength must have different meanings in the horoscope. A canon of planetary strength could be concocted quite randomly (as indeed some of them, such as the terms, seem to have been) and an appropriate doctrine of interpretation conjured up to fit. We have an example of this in the use of two different and contradictory zodiacs which nonetheless utilize the same scheme of essential dignities. Yet these contradictory schemes of dignities all seem to work for the individual practitioners who use them.

Morinus' technique is based mostly on the houses, and prediction of how the affairs of a house will go depends upon the strength of the planets:

1)   occupying that house
2)   ruling that house, and
3)   occupying the opposite house

(in that order).

While following this fundamental guideline, the interpretations given in this book are based upon the plerophory that good or ill fortune in the world is a reflection of the native's inner state (personality factors) – that 'Character is Destiny', that 'You create your own reality'. Thus, disorderly conditions in love relationships may be shown by a weak Venus or weak 7th house planets, but they arise from something going on inside the native.

The chief point on which Morinus and I differ is in the matter of ascribing general signification to the planets. To Morinus, the local determination (the condition of the particular house involved in a matter – e.g. 4th for the father or 7th for the marriage) is all-important in determining the good or ill fortune to be expected in specific life situations and relationships: "The Sun does not have an influence on earth ... except very generally, but not specifically – as on the health, profession, etc. – because no such specific influence exists except that which is brought about through house-location in the horoscope." [Morinus Book 21, page 6]. Again, "Astrologers have always assumed in considering the essential determinations of a planet that the Sun, for example, would signify the father, the husband, kings, nobles, fame, prestige, and the health, etc. ... But because this analogy is based on the essential nature of the Sun and the influence of the Sun is completely universal and indifferent, the Sun could not by analogy alone indicate the health any more than it could the father, the husband, the king, or the position. ... One could not assume that the Sun specifically means one of these things any more than another. ... (But) if it happens that these determinations through the houses refer to things to which the planet has an analogy, the resulting effect will take place with considerable certainty." [Morinus Book 21, pages 11-13].

On this point I must gainsay Morinus in holding that the planets of themselves – and particularly pairs of planets related by aspect – do indeed signify specific worldly matters. Thus, Morinus would say that the Sun only signifies the father if it is located in or rules the 4th house; Venus only signifies marriage if it is located in or rules the 7th house, etc. I hold that the Sun can indeed signify the parent (and Sun-Saturn aspects have particular reference to the father), and Venus (and Venus-Mars aspects in particular) can indeed signify intimate relationships, no matter what houses these planets are located in. In other words, if you want to know what a native's marriage prospects are, then by all means look at the 7th house (which actually will tell you more about the type of partner chosen than about how the marriage will go), but also take into account the condition of Venus, and particularly her aspects to or reception with Mars. **And then take the majority – the overall flavor – of the testimonies.** The stars incline – they do not compel, and astrological interpretation is ultimately a matter of *feeling* (not something you could ever computerize).

The Basic Keyword System

In the scheme of astrological interpretation which we will adopt here, each planet represents a different subpersonality, or thought form, of the native's overall personality. These subpersonalities can either be strengthened or weakened depending upon their good or bad celestial, terrestrial, or aspectual state:

Sun symbolizes the native's sense of **purpose**

Moon symbolizes the native's sense of **assurance**

Mercury symbolizes the native's **mentality**
Venus symbolizes the native's **enjoyment**
Mars symbolizes the native's sense of **accomplishment**
Jupiter symbolizes the native's **understanding**
Saturn symbolizes the native's sense of **responsibility**
Uranus symbolizes the native's sense of **independence**
Neptune symbolizes the native's **intuition**
Pluto symbolizes the native's **clarity**

In an attempt to answer the question of *how* these different subpersonalities are strengthened or weakened by the different types of strength (celestial, terrestrial, and aspectual), we will follow Dr. Marc Edmund Jones' classification scheme[4] of interpreting the difference between signs – houses – planets as being that between Function – Circumstances – Activity, respectively:

Function: Celestial state refers to the native's **attitude** towards him/herself and other people (which can either be **spirited** in good state versus **non-plussed** in bad state);

Circumstances: Terrestrial state refers to the native's **position** amongst other people (**dominating** when angular versus **reactive** when cadent);

Activity: Aspectual state refers to the native's **actions** with respect to other people, (**detached** when well-aspected versus **maladjusted** when afflicted).

These keywords, which appear in the Keywords Tables appended to each section, can be used to cobble together cookbook interpretations, but their main purpose is to be evocative and suggestive (as are the interpretations for the individual planets). For example, Saturn in good celestial state (strong by sign position) but bad terrestrial state (cadent) shows that the native's sense of **responsibility** is **spirited (conscientious)** but **reactive (vague)** – i.e. well-meaning, but not altogether there.

---

4. *The Essentials of Astrological Analysis* by Dr. Marc Edmund Jones, Sabian WA 1970. This book is as important a foundation document for the theory and practice of astrological interpretation as are the books of Morinus.

1

Celestial State

"One should not understand the benefic planets to be only Jupiter and Venus, but rather any planet (will be benefic) when well disposed by its celestial state: Mars and Saturn in such a (good) state acquire power to confer benefits, and, since the planets cannot put that ability to benefit into effect more so than in the benefic Houses, when they are posited there (in benefic Houses) we say that they are made fortunate by those (benefic) Houses." [Morinus Book 18, page 78].

Morinus considers that the two most important types of extrinsic planetary strength are *Celestial State* (dignity or debility due to zodiacal sign placement, also termed *Essential Dignity*) and *Terrestrial State* (angularity), in that order, [Morinus Book 18, pages 12, 14].

Let us take a look at how different planets respond to being located in the different signs. Consider, as an analogy, a group of tourists in New York City. Harry goes to see a Broadway show; Mary goes to Central Park; Joe goes to the stock exchange. The observed behavior is the result of individual temperament, not of New York City per se, which but provides a backdrop, or range of possibilities. A farm would provide a different range of possibilities: Harry and Joe might be really bored and frustrated there, but Mary would be in her element. Similarly, the signs provide a range of possibilities for the activity of the planets, and some signs are more harmonious with certain planets' inherent natures than are others. (See the Table of Essential Dignities at end of chapter).

As an example, consider the case of Venus. Venus is adept at creating opportunities, and some signs provide an ambience more favorable to this activity than others. But Venus will create opportunities no matter where she finds herself, only with greater difficulty in the more rigid, unyielding signs. For example, Venus in bad celestial state is controlling rather than playful, thus Venus in Virgo is picky, critical, never satisfied, and Venus in Scorpio is great in bed and ready to boogy any time, any place, but the sex is mechanical and egocentric – there's nothing tender or romantic about it. As another example, Mars butts his way through things, but experiences greater frustration in trying to do this in the softer, more sensitive and temporizing signs. The point is that the traits observed when a given planet is posited in a given sign will be a product principally of the planet, not of the sign.

We can take as a rule of thumb that a planet in bad celestial state is more vulnerable, confused or fuzzier. Bad celestial state renders the active planets (Sun-Mars-Saturn) passive and the passive planets (Moon-Venus) active. Morinus would concur in part with this notion: "(When a planet is) in exile its power is vitiated while in fall it is made weak and more inactive." [Morinus Book 21, page 75].

Mercury and Jupiter are more detached and mental – not classifiable as active or passive per se. We can say that good celestial state increases the definiteness of whatever a planet symbolizes, rendering it more flexible, adaptable, spontaneous, and alert to opportunities; whereas bad celestial state tends to be either more ambivalent or else more adamant – stiffer, more uncomfortable, missing opportunities. Thus, celestial state can be characterized as **attitude**: planets in good celestial state get the point; planets in bad celestial state miss the point (of the activity symbolized by the planet). Good celestial state shows an easy, effortless, positive attitude; whereas bad celestial state shows a self-conscious, labored, defensive attitude.

Morinus says that "When a planet is posited in its Domicile (a sign it rules), that planet acts only according to its own elemental nature but with twice its influential virtue." [Morinus Book 18, page 14]. Moreover, "When malefics (Mars, Saturn) occupy their Domiciles, they typically produce beneficial results in good Houses and are less damaging in the bad Houses." [Morinus Book 18, page 19].

Morinus considers that a planet in its exaltation sign is even more powerful than the planet in its Domicile: "Exaltation being the location most proportionate to its virtue and where it contains the most powerful virtue. A planet in Exaltation typically produces tremendous and sudden effects. ... The exalted planet acts forcefully and almost aggressively." [Morinus Book 18, page 17].

Per Morinus, "The opinion is widespread that a planet in domicile shows stability or indicates stable things; in exaltation – sudden and important changes; in triplicity – some association of meaning of the houses involved." [Morinus Book 21, page 73].

According to Morinus, planets in their detriment sign are "perverse": "A planet in its detriment acts according to its own nature and that of its dispositor, but in a depraved manner." [Morinus Book 18, page 20]. Where Morinus considers a planet in its detriment to be "corrupted", he considers a planet in its fall to be "debilitated": "A planet in its fall is quite weakened in its efforts to act according to its own nature." [Morinus Book 18, page 21].

Essentially dignified and debilitated planets point to the natives' chief spheres of interest and concern, their moments of heightened attentiveness and self-awareness (or self-consciousness, in the case of the debilities). Planets which are essentially dignified are **spirited**: they concentrate and direct energy; planets which are essentially debilitated are **non-plussed**: they dissipate energy. But peregrine (i.e. neither essentially dignified nor debilitated) planets operate in more of an automatic, perfunctory, taken-for-granted manner. For example, Mercury essentially dignified is serious-minded, self-controlled, and intent upon living up to some idealized image; whereas Mercury peregrine is perfunctory, unapologetic, and matter-of-fact. Mars essentially dignified is challenging, probing, analyzing, and intent upon proving its mettle; whereas Mars peregrine is accepting, credulous, and inclined to take things at face value. Dignified planets are operative in the native's most attentive moments; peregrine planets operate in the native's automatic-pilot moments.

When there is a **preponderance**[1] **of planets posited in their respective signs of essential dignity or debility**, then there is a weighting in the direction of increased self-awareness: you are conscientious, punctilious, intense. You usually try to give your best, but often feel overextended or put upon. You can be rather touchy or high-strung in temperament –

---

1. Six or more – Note: the definition of the term 'preponderance' depends upon frequency – thus for example we define 3 planets which are in their exaltation signs, or unaspected, or stationary, to constitute a 'preponderance'; whereas we require 4 planets in their ruling signs, or conjunct angles, to constitute a 'preponderance'. See Dr. Jones' Methodology in Appendix 2.

overly fastidious or a bit of the poseur – but you are always wide awake and alert to nuances.

On the other hand, when **all planets are peregrine**, what is indicated is nonchalance: you are relaxed, slow-paced, but rather desultory in your interests, lacking in real gusto for life. But because you have few axes to grind, you manage to get along quite well with all sorts of people.

Morinus considers that peregrine planets are somewhat weakened, but that "one must attend only to whether the planet lies in the sign of a friend or an enemy. … A peregrine planet in the home of a friend suffers hardly any diminution in its power to act according to its own nature …. On the other hand, if the planet occupies the home of an enemy, it becomes frustrated and malicious." [Morinus Book 18, page 21]. N.B: In contrast to Morinus, I would consider that any aspect which may exist between the planet and its dispositor[2] outweighs the innate friendship or enmity of the planet with its dispositor (especially since – except for the Moon and Saturn, Morinus and I disagree on which planets combine favorably or unfavorably). If there is no aspect with the dispositor, then the innate felicity or infelicity of the planetary combination can be considered (see the Table of Favorable and Unfavorable Planetary Combinations at the end of Chapter 3).

Morinus quotes Cardan's observations that "planets in their own Domiciles are more representative of the native's life, body, customary behavior, and mentality; planets in their Exaltations are more strongly connected with honors, dignity, actions, and changes of fortune; and planets in their Triplicities are more powerfully effective with regards to friendships and dialogues with others." [Morinus Book 18, page 23].

I would say that planets in their impersonal essential dignities (ruler and detriment) are somewhat detached in their view of life. They act in a cerebral manner and are very sensitive to any encroachment upon their prerogatives. Ruler is self-sufficient and dominates its sphere of activity, whereas detriment is dependent and in thrall to its environment. Planets in their impersonal dignities seek respect from or acknowledgement by other people, primarily. On the other hand, planets in their personal dignities (exaltation and fall) are completely absorbed in their own view of life. They are impulsive and whole-hearted (in

---

2. The planet which rules the sign in which the given planet is posited.

contrast to the judiciousness of the impersonal dignities); they throw themselves completely into what they are doing, and they aim to make the most of any opportunity. Exaltation is practical and in control of its sphere of activity; whereas fall is wistful, easily overwhelmed, and incapable of managing its affairs. Planets in their personal dignities seek fulfillment, primarily – they follow their own star (successfully in the case of exaltation and frustratingly in the case of fall) rather than seek acceptance or approval from other people.

If there are **more planets posited in their impersonal (ruler and detriment) dignities** than in their personal (exaltation and fall) dignities, then you are headstrong, self-willed, and intent. You tend to regard life as a challenge against which you must prove yourself. You have an inflated dignity and are less interested in concrete accomplishment or results than in your own personal performance and effectiveness in influencing the course of events. You can be heavy-handed and uncompromising, but are imbued with a strong sense of personal honor.

By contrast, if there are **more planets posited in their personal (exaltation and fall) dignities** than in their impersonal dignities, then you are irrepressible, imaginative, and experimentative, and are inclined to give full rein to your fancies. You regard life as an opportunity, and are usually off on your own tangent or living in a world of your own. You can be impervious, vague, or given to dabbling, but you are open to new ideas and suggestions and have a very unique perspective on life.

Planets in their positive essential dignities (ruler and exaltation) are highly accepting of themselves, forward-looking in their attitude, and smooth in their dealings with other people. They are poised and fully present in the now moment. Ruling planets have something of a sense of noblesse oblige or detachment; whereas exalted planets are more self-promoting and inclined to play life as a game. Exaltation is thoroughly practical, hence more resilient and opportunistic than ruler, which inclines to the notion that the world is at its service. Planets in their positive dignities don't permit themselves to become hampered by personal involvements: their egos are in good shape and they have little stake in outcomes beyond their control. They focus energy and waste little effort.

On the other hand, planets in their debilities (detriment and fall) are non-accepting of themselves, distrustful of their own feelings and instincts, hesitant in their outreach, and rather pessimistic in their outlook. Detriment has a sense of either isolation from or over-dependence on others, whereas fall is more histrionic, self-dramatizing, self-indulgent, overdone. Planets in their debilities indicate weak egos and a constant need for reassurance.

Natives **with a preponderance of planets essentially dignified** (5 or more in ruler and exaltation) are bold and self-certain, suave, and stylish. You contest issues with all your verve; yet you can take setbacks with relative equanimity. You are imperturbable and self-sufficient, deal with situations smoothly and impersonally, take things as they come. You don't permit yourself to be put out or touched too deeply. Albeit smug and remote, you are principled and idealistic, and always try to make the best of things.

On the other hand, a **preponderance of planets essentially debilitated** (5 or more in detriment and fall) indicates that you are self-conscious, nervous, and wary. Albeit sociable and outgoing, you are super-sensitive, easily hurt, and take things very much to heart. You shrink from reproach and placate or temporize wherever possible. You feel a strong need to be looked up to, and usually try to play the good fellow. You tend to be shy or awkward, but are genuinely unassuming and friendly.

When a **preponderance of planets** (4 or more) **are posited in their ruling signs** you possess an attitude of superiority, nobility of character, and a can-do spirit. You project a sense of loftiness or superiority. You decide for yourself where your responsibilities and commitments will lie, and you don't much bother yourself about anything else. Self-reliant and self-content – even a bit complacent – you can strike other people as being unduly stuffy or stiff. Yet on the positive side you are both idealistic and gracious, possessing an unimpeachable personal integrity.

When a **preponderance of planets** (4 or more) **are posited in their detriments,** then you tend to be defensive and self-protective. You are not so much self-effacing as unvarnished, rough around the edges, with an 'aw shucks' simplicity of manner and a lack of subtlety and diplomacy. You can be quite blunt and bluff – you don't especially try to make an impression on anyone. There may be a sense of effeteness or ennui about you, or a cantankerous pernicketiness. On your positive side, you are plainspoken, forthright, and truly solicitous for the well-being of others.

A **preponderance of planets** (3 or more) **posited in their exaltations** makes you insouciant, untrammeled, and willing to act in complete fidelity to your own instincts and desires. You are confident and imposing, shrewd and opportunistic. You take things as they come and can usually turn them to account. You are self-promoting and self-aggrandizing, but you are inimitably yourself at all times, and you grace your actions with a hallmark of personal touch and flair.

By contrast, **a preponderance of planets** (3 or more) **posited in their signs of fall** makes you insecure and uneasy, with an air of constant vigilance. You may put on a bit of a front since you never seem to just relax and let go. You tend to see yourself as a victim; or life as a series of bewildering maneuvers or dodges. You are somewhat sulky and inclined to labor your acts, but you are frank and aware of your limitations.

Keywords for Celestial State of Planets

Planet	Strengthens/ Weakens	Good State	Bad State
		Spirited	Non-plussed
Sun	Purpose	Resolute	Temporizing
Moon	Assurance	Secure	Susceptible
Mercury	Mentality	Clever	Adamant
Venus	Enjoyment	Ingratiating	Finicky
Mars	Accomplishment	Whole-hearted	Indecisive
Jupiter	Understanding	Disinterested	Preoccupied
Saturn	Responsibility	Conscientious	Prissy

Interpretations for Celestial State

"The aspects made by a planet in a bad celestial state will confer no benefit." [Morinus Book 18, page 22].

Sun in Good Celestial State = Spirited Purpose = Resolute

You are poised, self-possessed, and proud, with an aristocratic (autocratic) bearing and a sense that you belong in any milieu, and are on top of any situation in which you might find yourself. You are composed and in command of yourself, and are aboveboard and forthright in your dealings.

You have little native subtlety or gift for guile, so you are wary of (and confused by) nuances, and you bid for clear-cut situations and final solutions. Although you pride yourself on being eminently reasonable and impartial, and you believe you are acting in the best interests of all concerned, you usually take it for granted that things will be done *your* way. You are bold, outfront, and untrammeled by adversity.

Sun in Bad Celestial State = Non-Plussed Purpose = Temporizing
You are scrupulous, diligent, and possessed of a shrewd, adroit perspicacity. You tend to rely upon artfulness and cunning rather than directness to get your way with people. You are noncommittal, evasive, and try to skirt issues rather than to take the bull by the horns and confront things directly. Since you shy from involvement (and even challenge), you may lack an overriding sense of direction in life and just drift along, allowing the pull and tug of circumstances to decide major issues for you. You are often content to underachieve since you prefer compromise or going around whenever possible. Albeit naturally reserved, you have a friendly, disarming and non-threatening manner.

Moon in Good Celestial State = Spirited Assurance = Secure
You are self-composed and emotionally stable, and have a gracious, imperturbable personal manner. You are blasé, matter-of-fact, inclined to take things in your stride. You know what you want out of life, what makes you comfortable and what you can live with, and you are always able to feel at home. You possess an unflinching determination and considerable personal flair. You are not afraid to blaze new trails, nor move on to new things when old ones have exhausted their potentialities. Since you respond only to your own inner promptings, you can be disconcertingly cool, aloof, and unreachable in spite of your outward friendliness. You shine when you can bring your doggedness to bear upon the realization of a high ideal.

Moon in Bad Celestial State = Non-Plussed Assurance = Susceptible
You are rather sensitive and moody, with an air of disgruntlement or of being put-upon. You are testy, easily frustrated, and quick to take offense; your knee-jerk impulse always is to dig in your heels and close up into yourself. Since you are blunt, indelicate, and have a suspicious nature, you are something of a misfit and you often feel alienated and

isolated from other people. Although you are more practical and self-serving than idealistic, you possess a bumbling, unaffected naiveté and unvarnished sincerity which endears you to other people.

Mercury in Good Celestial State = Spirited Mentality = Clever
You are thoughtful, reflective, and possess good judgment and common sense. Even when worried you maintain a cool, collected façade. You brim with good advice, possess a genuine spirit of optimism, enjoy problem-solving, and believe that everything will work out for the best if allowed to take its natural course. You are a good listener and are eager to learn; you are confident in the soundness of your own perspicacity (which on the negative side can become a complacent self-satisfaction). You possess a true intellectual curiosity and an interest in other people and their points of view.

Mercury in Bad Celestial State = Non-Plussed Mentality = Adamant
You are bluff and blustery and are often more interested in making your point rather than in an effective give-and-take. You feel at pains to make sure that you are listened to and heeded, and you rely upon stonewalling or shutting down communications when you are not. You have strong opinions and you take them and yourself very seriously. In contrast to the mental agility and acuity of Mercury in its ruling signs, you tend to be overly rationalizing and ruminating, with something of a siege mentality. You often feel isolated, misjudged, in need of a little appreciation for your efforts, and can be quite huffy in demanding same. On the positive side you are outspoken and have a straightforward manner and a strong sense of duty.

Venus in Good Celestial State = Spirited Enjoyment = Ingratiating
You are irrepressible and irreverent, with a knowing eye, a mischievous smile, and a childlike sense of fun. You possess an open and inviting manner which puts people at their ease and you are unabashedly yourself at all times. Albeit sociable and outgoing, you are independent emotionally and may have an unconventional or Bohemian streak. You are sensitive and perceptive, but generally prefer comfort to sacrifice, and either you eschew worldly success, or else you pursue it by means of adroitness rather than effort. You are eternally hopeful and positive in your outlook.

Venus in Bad Celestial State = Non-Plussed Enjoyment = Finicky
You are prickly and thin-skinned, with an air of haughtiness or fastidiousness, and you need everything *just so*. You often feel ill-at-ease with other people, and are rather distrustful of just relaxing and letting things happen or unfold on their own. You can be moody and snappish, with a dominating presence, and you quite consciously control and manipulate relationships (or try to). You have strong convictions which can make you too set in your likes and dislikes to appreciate life's little surprises. On the positive side you are punctilious in the discharge of what you consider your responsibilities to be.

Mars in Good Celestial State = Spirited Accomplishment = Whole-Hearted
You are self-certain, cocky, and quick to act and react. You dislike shilly-shallying; you just get down to brass tacks and plunge on ahead. You know exactly where you stand and what you'll stand for, even if it means going it alone. You welcome challenge and the chance to prove your mettle, and your insight tends to be quite apropos. On the negative side you can be rather blunt and short, with an autocratic self-will and a lack of subtlety and delicacy.

Mars in Bad Celestial State = Non-Plussed Accomplishment = Indecisive
You are doubtful, unsure of yourself, and easily frustrated. You try to be pleasing, to fit and trim, to avoid making waves, and as a result you are easily imposed upon or taken advantage of (or feel that you are). You are vague and perfunctory in relationship and you have a tendency to smolder rather than to speak up and speak out. When you do finally assert yourself, you are liable to exaggerate, to take unwarranted umbrage, or to insist upon making your point or raising an issue where there really isn't any need to. "(Mars in Cancer) makes me quick to anger but also makes it easy for me to restrain myself. In addition, I become remiss at times when I should avenge myself." [Morinus Book 18 page 26]. You rely upon dogged and obstinate persistence rather resourcefulness and dash to get your way.

Jupiter in Good Celestial State = Spirited Understanding = Disinterested
You are good-natured, humorous and open-minded, with a broad,

philosophical take on your fellow humans and the passing scene. You are relatively imperturbable, holding yourself above unnecessary contention or pother and trying to avoid becoming entangled or bogged down by circumstances. You take all viewpoints into account, but you try to think things through and come to your own conclusions. You are tolerant and avuncular, with a natural sympathy. Although you tend to see yourself as the impartial observer, you do rather expect that others will defer to your judgment, and you can be infuriatingly complacent, patronizing, and remote. Yet you are always sincere, have a unique outlook on life and reach for depth of understanding.

Jupiter in Bad Celestial State = Non-Plussed Understanding = Preoccupied

Although you are outgoing and affable, your gaiety is a bit studied or forced. You are actually not very relaxed or at ease around people, and seem abstracted and not fully present. You are at pains to express yourself clearly, however you tend to dwell upon yourself, or to think about what you will say next, rather than to listen sympathetically to the feelings of others. While you are quite chatty, your conversation tends to be a repetition of the same homilies or pat ideas. You strongly need to feel yourself to be in the right at all times, so you readily shift from trying to be pleasant and pleasing to being short and brusque. On the positive side you are readily approachable and truly try to do your best.

Saturn in Good Celestial State = Spirited Responsibility = Conscientious

You are calm, level-headed, and tend to take things in your stride. You roll up your sleeves and get down to whatever it is that needs to be done, with little protest or wasted effort. You take pride in your competence and dedication rather than demand any special privileges for yourself. You relish challenge and have a can-do manner and natural superiority – a sense that you are anyone's equal, and that you can hold your own with the best of them. You are impartial, judicious, and possess a democratic sense of justice and fair play. You are a good listener, and you inspire trust because of your sincerity, straightforwardness, and unvarnished simplicity of manner.

Saturn in Bad Celestial State = Non-Plussed Responsibility = Prissy
You are rather easily frustrated and put-upon, and jealously guard your personal prerogatives. You have a tendency to prance and preen – to think that you're hot stuff, or at least worthy of special consideration and recognition. You are demonstrative and self-justifying, with a strong need to continually prove yourself and to win (or compel) the respect of others. There can at times be a vain, petty posturing, or a wrong-headed contrariety. On your positive side you're not afraid to speak out and to call a spade a spade.

Table of Essential Dignities and Debilities of the Planets

Planet	Ruler	Detriment	Exaltation	Fall
Sun	LE	AQ	AR	LI
Moon	CN	CP	TA	SC
Mercury	GE - VI	SG - PI	VI	PI
Venus	LI - TA	AR - SC	PI	VI
Mars	AR - SC	LI - TA	CP	CN
Jupiter	SG - PI	GE - VI	CN	CP
Saturn	CP-AQ	CN - LE	LI	AR
Node			GE	SG

UR-NE-PL (the essential dignities are not applied to the modern planets)

Sole Dispositor

"By this consideration one always clearly knows which planet or planets at any given moment are the most powerful in the heavens or in the whole world – because the planets that are located in their own Domiciles are dispositors (planetary rulers) of the other planets; and if two planets are in their respective Domiciles and are the dispositors of the rest, they will also be very powerful." [Morinus Book 18, page 19].

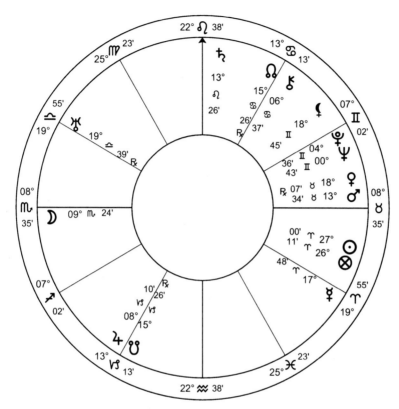

Charlie Chaplin: 16 April 1889, 20.00 GMT, London, England.
51N30 00W10

A sole dispositor occurs in a horoscope when one – and only one –
planet lies in its ruling sign, and all the other planets lie in signs which,
by a series of removes in rulership (disposition), work back to that ruling
planet. For example, in the horoscope of Charlie Chaplin, Venus is the
sole dispositor because it is in its own sign, Taurus; Venus disposes of
Mars and Uranus (since they are in signs ruled by Venus – Taurus and
Libra, respectively); in the same way, Mars disposes of the Sun, Mercury
in Aries and the Moon in Scorpio; the Sun disposes of Saturn in Leo;
Saturn disposes of Jupiter in Capricorn; and Mercury disposes of Neptune
and Pluto in Gemini. Thus all planets, by a series of dispositions, work
back to Venus.

A sole dispositor in a horoscope is the sign of the self-made person:
one who stands apart from family and social milieu and has achieved

something quite different from what you might expect from knowing his or her background and upbringing.

In a sense we can say that all the other planets bow down to the sole dispositor, and indeed it is often the case that natives who have a sole dispositor expect other people to bow down to them. If you have a sole dispositor in your horoscope, then you have a way of turning deadly earnest in order to structure a social situation on your own terms. You might say things like, "All kidding aside, let's cut across and get down to brass tacks." What this means is, "Let's do it *my* way." You have a strong sense of personal dignity which cannot take derision; to poke fun at you is to stab you in your very bowels, yet your staunchly individualistic slant on life and highly original point of view insure that you will be taken seriously.

Sole dispositor natives usually find their early years frustrating and unfulfilling. If you have a sole dispositor, it is very difficult for you to adjust yourself to the demands of the people around you; instead you expect them to adjust to you. You are the proverbial round peg in a square hole. Because you cannot fit yourself into the established mold, you compensate by nurturing dreams of a grander destiny than what you view as the pedestrian concerns of your associates. You cannot accept the values and choices that you find being made for your life by your family, society, and peers; you find no repose in what everyone else is taking for granted. You are often torn with self-doubt, and from an early age are forced to rely upon your own inner resources for satisfaction rather than on the support and rewards which accrue by obeying the rules. You become feisty, pugnacious, and easily frustrated – an emotionally distant and detached person who answers to no one but yourself and who brooks no interference in your life. If the horoscope is otherwise afflicted, the lack of understanding and positive feedback received from your environment in your youth may cause you to carry a residue of bitterness into adulthood.

It is with maturity that you come into full possession of your powers, with the realization that you can become the author of your own rules. By this point you have developed an unflinching determination which approaches bullheadedness; a singleness of purpose or point of view, a self-obsession which is untrammeled by the considerations (such as appearances, security, or conventional morality) that inhibit other people. You become a law unto yourself. There can be a tyrannical or absolutist streak, but at the same time a fearless and uncompromising integrity, conscientiousness, and diligence.

It is rare to find a sole dispositor native who is really at peace. There is usually a driving engine – restless ambition or need for vindication – and an intolerance for any sort of stricture. The people who know you tend to see you as being alternately a bastion of moral courage and a petty dictator.

Although you feel like a lone wolf, you nonetheless make constant demands on the attention and attentiveness of other people. You love to teach or lecture in order to keep the focus of attention on yourself. You have a strong need to feel in control of things, a step or two ahead of everyone else. And while there might be a simplistic, good-versus-evil or us-versus-them taint to your worldview, your vision of life does tend to be broader or more idealistic than that of your fellows. Moreover you're quite ready to fight and die for your beliefs. There is a nobility of character and a sense of command about you – a uniqueness or genius all your own which compels the genuine respect (if not subservience) of other people.

Sun sole dispositor is the most candid and artless of the sole dispositor types – and therefore perhaps the subtlest. You have a childlike desire to shine in the world, together with a childish exhibitionism and an inclination to tantrums when you feel neglected. In other words, with this dispositor you possess all the characteristics of Leo in exaggerated form: the regal, lofty pride together with the paper-thin ego which is so easily scratched and hurt. You succeed by projecting a naïve innocence which arouses the protective instincts of other people, and disposes them to indulge or overlook your overblown vanity and flagrant egotism. Your moves and power plays are so blatantly obvious and unabashedly theatrical that no one really feels threatened by them, and hence no one seriously opposes them. You win people over with a hearty sense of amusement with both life and yourself, and with a spirited *joie de vivre*.

Moon sole dispositor occurs rarely, and I have seen so few examples of it in my practice that I would not care to hazard a guess as to its meaning. Some examples are: Julian Huxley, Anne Morrow Lindbergh, Liza Minelli, and Igor Stravinsky.

Mercury sole dispositor is the most amiable of the sole dispositor types and is the one most involved in group ventures. Outgoing and friendly, you make a point of keeping things calm and sociable. In fact, you can carry your imperturbability to maddening lengths. You are a good listener, giving other people your full attention and concern, and smoothing out any differences of opinion. Yet you always maintain your space and distance, and you have a knack for getting on a personal basis with people without actually becoming intimate or committed. You depend for much of your success on other people's good faith and tractability, relying upon your patient reasonableness to sway them. You present yourself as the impartial expert or arbiter, one who has no emotional stake in the proceedings but merely wishes to see things carried out in good order – i.e. your way. You win people over with your dry sense of humor and radiant good cheer.

Venus sole dispositor is the most overtly compliant and conciliatory of the sole dispositor types. You are kindly and solicitous for the feelings of other people without letting yourself become too involved with them. You shy away from any sort of disharmony or fuss, and thus can be amicable without being intimate, and sympathetic without being warm. You cut yourself off from the emotional ties which produce ups and downs in other people, yet you have a dark, brooding side which often sucks other people into your moods. You succeed by maintaining your own equilibrium in the face of disharmony, by refusing to be drawn into conflicts which dissipate your energy. You emerge from strife as fresh as a daisy, having worn everyone else down to a frazzle. Yet you have a pleasant, unruffled disposition and a cool serenity which wins the respect of all the people around you.

Mars sole dispositor is the most intense of the sole dispositor types. Although you possess great personal charm and élan, you have an overriding need to feel in the right and have the final word. You thrive on contention and throw down your gauntlet at the slightest provocation. You can muster a formidable array of justifications and rationalizations, Talmudic in their intricacy and Koranic in their inflexibility, to meet any argument or plea. You depend for your success on the inertia of others, gladly taking up responsibilities which they drop or avoid, and thereby augmenting your own power. You don't shrink from tasks which are dirty, dangerous, or dull, so long as you can execute them without interference or the need for compromise. You manage to avoid seriously antagonizing people – and indeed, win their indulgence if not their support – with your quixotic optimism, youthful cockiness, and readiness to tackle anything.

Jupiter sole dispositor is the most humanitarian of the sole-dispositor types, the most concerned with people en masse and with standards of fairness and abstract justice. Because you tend to see yourself as a victim, you assume the role of protector and defender of the helpless and oppressed; a bulwark of rectitude in a world without conscience, a mother hen in a world full of hawks. You succeed by identifying feelings and concerns with the moral right, thereby expanding your power by defending an ethical principle, and pursuing personal interests under a rubric of disinterestedness. Although you are self-effacing and mild of manner, you are far, far from being humble; when aroused you can be as tough and adamant as any sole dispositor type. You win people over with your high idealism, ingratiating manner, and true sincerity.

Saturn sole dispositor is the shrewdest, most calculating of the sole dispositor types. You carry out your empire-building in the most deliberate, step-by-step fashion, and yet caution has no part in your make-up. You possess an uncompromising dignity and a stone-faced determination which hardens as the odds mount against you. You have nerves of iron and a calm, unhurried manner in situations where most people would be biting their nails. You take a rather cynical view of human nature, and uphold a strong sense of personal competence and superiority. You depend for success on the confusion of other people; you know you can wait them out, or else exploit their doubts and hesitation with a rapid, bold stroke. Your greatest asset is your pride in your own fitness and complete self-dedication to everything you do.

2

Terrestrial State

"First: the four angular Houses (1, 10, 7, and 4) are inherently more powerful than the other Houses." [Morinus Book 18, page 73]. "Next in strength to the Ascendant comes the Midheaven, then the Descendant, and finally the Imum Coeli." [Morinus Book 18, page 74]. "The angular Houses take precedence [in strength] over the succedent ones, and these in turn over the cadent Houses." [Morinus Book 18, page 76].

The disposition of the planets with respect to the circle of the houses gives rise to the dignity of *Terrestrial State*, or propinquity to one of the four angles of the birth chart: Ascendant (Asc), Midheaven (MC), Descendant (Desc) and Nadir (or *Imum Coeli*, IC). Terrestrial state refers to the natives' approach to social relationships. A planet posited in an angular house (1st, 4th, 7th, 10th) tends to find social relationships stimulating; a planet posited in a succedent house (2nd, 5th, 8th, 11th) tends to find social relationships challenging; a planet posited in a cadent house (3rd, 6th, 9th, 12th) tends to find social relationships overwhelming. Angular planets do not indicate favorable relationships (which is shown by being well-aspected) so much as an easy control of relationships – an ability (symbolized by the particular planet) to land on one's feet and dominate the proceedings. Cadent planets, by contrast, are more in thrall or in bondage to their social relationships – these planets bring a schooling in self-denial or renunciation.

Terrestrial strength – more than any other type of dignity – is a measure of adaptation to social conditioning. Where celestial strength is inborn – a gleam in the eye – terrestrial strength refers to learned strategies of social dominance. Angularity is not merely a matter of social skill. It also implies a certain take on everyday society – thoroughness, leaving nothing to chance or happenstance, enforcing one's own will rather than just crossing one's fingers and hoping for the best (as most people do). Therein inures the real strength of an angular planet: *taking complete responsibility for the proceedings.*

In general, society trains people to shut up and obey blindly; to take as little initiative and personal responsibility as possible. However, some people – at least in some areas of their lives (shown by their angular planets) – come to the realization that it's all just a game, that the game *does* have rules, and that those rules can be manipulated to advantage. Often this knowledge is learned from rather singular parents, who tended to make or break the rules themselves. This is perhaps why Gauquelin found that "children tended to have the same angular planets as their parents, especially if the latter's were just past the Rising Point or MC."[1]

> "Observe whether a planet is in the angular, succedent, or cadent houses; for planets in the angles indicate effects which are continuous – especially when also in the fixed signs ... But in cadent houses and moveable signs the planets indicate things which are unstable; in the succedent houses the effects are intermediate." [Morinus Book 21, page 94].

In any given area of life, most people are milling around aimlessly, waiting for someone to tell them what to do, and there's a small minority of people giving all the orders. These latter people are symbolized in astrology as those who have angular planets. Actually, angular-planet people don't know much more about what's happening than anyone else, but they *seem* to: they have a facility for projecting the impression that they know what they're doing. There's a self-assurance and economy to their actions that induce other people to defer to them and cede them the lead.

Angularity symbolizes a sense of belonging, of being in the know, on the inside track. Angular types are not unconventional, but rather are above convention. They go through the motions of meeting – indeed, exceeding – social expectations, but they put very little importance upon appearances. They are aware (as most people are not) that social

---

1. Geoffrey Dean, *Recent Advances in Natal Astrology*, Astrological Association 1977, page 391.

conventions and expectations are wholly arbitrary and not to be taken too seriously. Therefore, they are able to make social role-playing a joyous, fulfilling, fruitful activity, rather than an onerous or daunting enterprise (as it seems to cadent planet people).

Practically everyone is personally ambitious. What distinguishes angular types from the rest is their understanding that there is a science to life – a technology for getting what you want. They don't sit around waiting for their 'lucky break' to drop down from heaven, nor do they just put in the time while slowly moving up the ranks. They intuit that life is a game, with definite rules – definite steps and decisions that can be made to succeed in the game. Where most people obey the rules, or more accurately, stumble around in the dark trying to figure out what the rules are, angular types *make* the rules.

Angular types possess a talent for self-promotion, not in an officious way, but with a definite noblesse oblige. In contrast to the strength conferred upon planets by virtue of their being posited in their ruling or exaltation signs, angular planets exhibit little exuberance or effusiveness. They possess a natural self-control which arises not so much from discipline as from a sense of ease, patience, and forbearance – a sense that life is at one's service, so there is no need to be pushy or overreaching. There is nothing blatant or indelicate about angular planets; their energy is not expended needlessly in demonstrativeness or attitudinizing, but is conserved, held back in reserve until needed. All angular planets make for a hard, cold practicality – even the so-called 'nice' planets (Moon, Venus, Jupiter) are nice only because that is the easiest way to manipulate people and get one's own way with them.

People with angular planets are the winners in life because they make that assumption – that they are winners. And because it's lonely at the top, angular planets also indicate a certain solitude and isolation. If those with angular planets quite consciously manipulate people and make decisions for the group, they also understand the responsibility that this entails.

Angular planets give people that sense of easy self-assurance associated with being a member of the ruling class. In earlier ages this meant membership in the aristocracy; in today's meritocracy it shows the educated and upwardly mobile as well as those born in the upper classes of society. People born in the upper classes have a winning attitude inculcated into them from birth (that they 'belong', that they are destined to rule), which is why angularity is associated with high social class and success in life. The members of the upper classes were historically the people who were 'bred' to lead and succeed.

Of course, there are always wealthy and upper-class natives who have no angular planets. These are the ones on whom this born-to-command-and-control-one's-destiny attitude doesn't stick or fit properly. They turn it into an attitude of snobbery, or one that says that life owes them a living. In other words, although exposed to the 'angular' attitude by virtue of their upbringing, they fail to catch the meaning of what a natural sense of prowess, adequacy, and leadership actually entails. They understand the superficial trappings of angularity (success) without grasping its essence (personal responsibility).

By the same token, there have always been instances of people born in the lower social classes who by sheer gumption raised themselves up in life in spite of all handicaps. The people with no angular planets who 'make it' on their own in a big way don't contradict the theory; all this means is that these people made it even without a native sense of fitness to command. Perhaps they stumbled into the limelight; or maybe they did it through driving ambition, determination, and force of will. In any case, this success will be found to have been accomplished as a freak of nature, or else as a tour de force, rather than as the end result of a natural process of unfoldment. It means that these natives' success in life was not the end result of a conscious sense of fitness but rather was the result of extraordinary talent, effort, or luck. In other words, success *can* come in spite of an absence of angular planets, but in that case the native has to work harder, or hit the right combination of fortuitous circumstances, in order to get the same effect.

It must also be noted that angularity shows nothing of the degree of success attained in life – whether the native set his or her sights high, or aimed for a comfortable niche; whether big success was attained with little pother, or at the cost of great sacrifice and suffering; indeed, whether success was actually attained, or whether the native went crashing down in flames. This sort of information is shown by benefic/malefic angular planets, and by how well-aspected or afflicted they are.

The angular houses are houses of action, whereas the cadent houses are houses of thought. Angular planets *do*, whereas cadent planets hold back and watch rather than jump in and stir things up. Thus, being cadent isn't as bad a debility for mental planets such as Mercury and Jupiter as it is for active planets like the Sun and Mars. What is shown by terrestrial state is how the native interacts in social groups – as a leader or follower, and in what ways. Angular planets are puppet masters, or Pied Pipers, who have everyone dancing to their tune. In one fashion or another (shown by the particular planet) angular planets maintain the upper hand: their position is **dominating**, whereas that of cadent planets is **reactive**. The particular planet involved indicates *how* the native interacts (e.g. in a Mercurial, Jovial, Saturnine fashion); and the particular angle involved indicates in what type of social group the native interacts in that fashion.

Angular planets symbolize strategies of control, and the four angles symbolize four different types of social relationships: casual, face-to-face relationships (Ascendant); formal and group relationships (Midheaven); intimate relationships and partnerships (Descendant); and standing alone (Nadir). Here we are only concerned with the dignity of angularity as a strength factor, not with what individual angles or planets conjunct the same mean in terms of personality factors, which will be discussed at the end of this chapter.

As an example, I have Jupiter rising in my natal chart and I am very generous with and appreciative of people, and I am always able to understand their viewpoint (whether I agree with them or not). However, this is just a conscious tactic to disarm people, win their trust, and make them dependent on me, rather than being a truly heartfelt and sympathetic impulse of benevolence. Sometimes people who have tried to tell me what to do have been blown away by how cold, hard, and utterly ruthless I can be (since I also have Sun, Saturn, and Pluto conjunct on the MC), but they foolishly believed my Jupiter-rising mask of being the nice guy. And, that stellium of planets on the MC is just another mask – a violent temper thing designed to scare people off (which it does), to force them to back down and leave me alone (since I also have Moon on the IC).

"Saturn, when unfortunate by its celestial state in the 1st or the 10th House, because of that [House placement], will be much more noxious for the essential significations of those Houses. Thus, when

Ptolemy said that planets in the angles are greatly fortified, this must be understood as being strengthened either to benefit or to do harm." [Morinus Book 18, page 78].

Take Saturn as an example: Saturn controls by fiat and fear – by sheer adamancy. Thus when on the Ascendant, Saturn is cold, gruff, and forbidding. Saturn conjunct the Midheaven moves unerringly into power vacuums to seize command. Saturn on the Descendant makes for obstinate or absent partners and difficult partnerships (planets conjunct the Descendant project their nature onto the partner – i.e. describe the type of partner chosen). And Saturn on the Nadir closes up into itself and goes its own way. Thus the Asc and MC can be considered active and the Desc and IC passive in their operation. The planets other than Saturn operate similarly, according to their respective natures: Sun on any angle disarms by self-assurance and forthrightness; Moon conjunct an angle is vulnerable and puts all its cards on the table; Mercury on an angle is glib and convincing; Venus conjunct an angle is gracious and accommodating; Mars conjunct an angle butts ahead and insists on its own way; Jupiter plays the impartial arbiter. All of these are bids for control, and the particular arena of control is shown by the particular angle (Asc = superficial, tête-à-tête relations; MC = formal and group relations; Desc = intimate relations; IC = solitude).

Let us, for present purposes, define a planet to be angular if it lies within a range of 5° of longitude before that angle to 15° after it. We will define a planet to be cadent if it lies within a range of from 15° before an angle to 35° degrees before it. This tactic – defining 'cadent' in terms of distance in longitude before the succeeding angle – sidesteps the problem of defining which house system to use (although it could be argued that this defaults to the Equal House System). Also, by specifying 20° rather than 30° ranges, we sidestep the question of the exact point where cadent turns into angular, and thus can keep distinctions as distinct as possible.

Angular planets have an angle: they have a come-on, a spiel. They are like used-car salesmen – in one way or another, they are selling themselves. Angular planets show a technique of self-promotion (depending upon the particular planet). Angular planets usually manage to land on their feet, and to dominate or capitalize on their situation.

If you have a **preponderance of angular planets** (4 or more) then you have an air of sublime self-assurance and a quiet bravado. You are shrewd, calculating, Machiavellian. You project the sense that you are in possession of yourself, can handle yourself in any circumstances, and you want everyone to know it. You can be unduly self-absorbed at times and affect an aloof benevolence, but you possess a unique point of view and love to demonstrate your skill. In the context of an afflicted chart this usually means that you feel a constant need to prove yourself and demonstrate your prowess and superiority – you play to the gallery. In a well-aspected chart it means you tend to insulate or isolate yourself – to go your own way and do your own thing, making as few waves as possible.

Having **no angular planets** means that you have no angles, no come-ons. You are not trying to set the world on fire or impress anybody. This is not to say that you are particularly humble or self-effacing, but there is a certain hesitancy about you, a willingness to just go along. You are low key, bland, easy-going, hail-fellow-well-met. You lead a conventional life, don't get ruffled, or make waves, and tend to be content with your lot. On your positive side you are artless, unaffected, unvarnished, and plainspoken. You're a straight shooter – a simple person – what people see is what they get. You're not trying to sell anybody anything, nor are you driven by a need to have other people see you as successful. You tend to conform to what is expected of you by your social milieu and you do your job as well as you can – you do not call special attention to yourself.

Interpretations for Terrestrial State

Sun Angular: Dominating Purpose = Self-Possessed

You are positive, self-certain, and hold your head up high. You have a cool, impersonal, and aloof manner – a noblesse oblige which confidently assumes its rightful place in any group, and simply assumes the approval or approbation of others. At times you can be overly supercilious, with an annoyingly smug insouciance. But you are noble and idealistic, and always brim with a cocky optimism.

Keywords for Terrestrial State of Planets

Planet	Strengthens/ Weakens	Angular	Cadent
		Dominating	Reactive
Sun	Purpose	Self-possessed	Defensive
Moon	Assurance	Poised	Solipsistic
Mercury	Mentality	Convincing	Awkward
Venus	Enjoyment	Spontaneous	Calculating
Mars	Accomplishment	Plucky	Malcontent
Jupiter	Understanding	Enthusiastic	Cautious
Saturn	Responsibility	Firm	Vague
Uranus	Independence	Outspoken	Cagey
Neptune	Intuition	Certain	Worried
Pluto	Clarity	Uncompromising	Doubtful

Sun Cadent: Reactive Purpose = Defensive

You are somewhat insecure and unsure of yourself, never quite positive that you are standing on firm ground. Therefore, your proposals and responses tend to miss their mark, being either too timid or too bumptious. You are overly dependent upon other people's opinions to assess your own status, so you sometimes strike others as being histrionic or overdone – not knowing when it's time to stop fishing for approval. Although it is difficult for you to admit error, you nonetheless try to stave off reproach by pulling your full share of the load.

Moon Angular: Dominating Assurance = Poised

You are self-possessed, unaffected, and can always find a way to relax and be yourself in any group situation. You have a nonjudgmental manner and are a sympathetic listener, so others find your presence reassuring. You can take major setbacks with relative equanimity, and you possess an eternal hopefulness and the ability to see beyond present disappointments to keep alive to new possibilities. Though you can be a bit condescending and above-it-all, you are the voice of calm reason in any group.

Moon Cadent: Reactive Assurance = Solipsistic
You have a nervous, flighty energy and are often out of synch, or unduly self-conscious with other people. Your constant focus is on your own feelings and point of view, therefore you can be rather unaccommodating and unreachable, and easily sidetracked by minor issues. You are overly picky and critical, and may nourish unreal expectations or inflated hopes, so you are quick to feel disappointed or discomfited. On your positive side you are scrupulous, punctilious, and attentive to details.

Mercury Angular: Dominating Mentality = Convincing
You are blithe, insouciant, and glib; and you go your own way with nary a fair-thee-well. You possess an unruffled and good-humored manner and you have implicit faith in your own fitness. You are a good listener and even better talker, and you win people over with your aplomb, frankness, and sincerity. You tend to play the impartial arbiter or disinterested referee in any group. Although usually tuned in to your own wavelength and rather captivated by your own adroitness, you are optimistic and forward-looking.

Mercury Cadent: Reactive Mentality = Awkward
You are socially bumbling and not altogether sure of where you stand. Communication is difficult for you since you put all your cards on the table and let the chips fall where they may, which can make you brusque, tart, and tactless. Albeit gregarious and outgoing, you jealously safeguard your personal interests from encroachment, and always see to it that you get your fair share of the pie. But you always speak your mind and fearlessly stick up for yourself no matter what.

Venus Angular: Dominating Enjoyment = Spontaneous
You are free-spirited and pleasure-loving – the wellspring of delight in any group. You have a courteous, disarming manner; you turn aside from unpleasantness and negativity and dwell upon the positive. You are something of a visionary, are emotionally self-sufficient, and are determined to enjoy yourself come what may. At times you can be unduly self-indulgent and delighted with yourself, but you are simple and unpretentious, and have an infectious sense of fun.

Venus Cadent: Reactive Enjoyment = Calculating
You tend to be pushy and insistent – always looking out for your own

self-interest and maintaining a constant vigilance over your rights and prerogatives. Your sociability tends to miss the mark: either you hold back, or else you tend to overdo the stubborn contentiousness bit. On your positive side you are scrupulous about doing your part and living up to (even exceeding) other people's expectations.

Mars Angular: Dominating Accomplishment = Plucky

You have a very original point of view and slant on life, and you express yourself candidly and fearlessly. Self-assured and devil-may-care, you go your own way and do your own thing without relying upon other people's approval or support, and by improvising whatever is needed. Although your self-confidence can verge on self-congratulations, you always stick to your guns, and you are inimitably yourself at all times.

Mars Cadent: Reactive Accomplishment = Malcontent

You are caustic and opinionated, and are somewhat inelegant or gauche in expressing yourself. You are easily misunderstood – or feel that you are – and are skeptical of other people's motives. You have a sense of being weary, overburdened, or bogged down by circumstances, and at your wits' end over other people. On your positive side you are punctilious and dutiful in carrying out your responsibilities.

Jupiter Angular: Dominating Understanding = Enthusiastic

You are idealistic and headstrong – even brash – in manner, and you always say what you're thinking. You disarm people with your naïve and bouncy self-assurance and considerable personal flair, and you are good at charming and wheedling people to get your way. You are optimistic and hopeful even in defeat, and are therefore able to take advantage of whatever opportunities arise. You impress and inspire others with your vitality and verve.

Jupiter Cadent: Reactive Understanding = Cautious

You are somewhat heavy-handed and slow to swing into action. You have to think things through and watch your step, making sure that you are always prepared and in a defensible position. Rather pigheaded and adamant, you rely upon inflexibility rather than finesse to win other people over. You try to convince people the way you try to convince yourself: by making appeals to reasonableness or abstract standards of fair play, and you feel rather put out when those rules don't work. On your positive side you are sober-minded and dogged at maintaining your position.

Saturn Angular: Dominating Responsibility = Firm

You are practical, well-grounded, and know how to stand up for yourself: other people are disinclined to challenge or tangle with your hardnosed immovability. Albeit stubborn and independent, you are at the same time realistic and skilled in the art of the possible. You have strong principles which you will not compromise under any circumstances, but you are willing to examine your position objectively and take other people's viewpoints into account in your calculations. You are enterprising, adventurous, and fearless in blazing new trails through life.

Saturn Cadent: Reactive Responsbility = Vague

You are never quite sure of your ground and thus you tend to trim and temporize, or else to put your foot down and stonewall. Because you take things to heart you don't assert yourself effectively, nor know how to deal with criticism or opposition. You tend to make issues where there's really no need to: you either get huffy and feel offended, or else you close your eyes and ears and charge over other people's sensibilities. You try to dodge blame by hedging your bets and leaving yourself an out, but you are quick to regain your composure and spring back up quickly after every stumble.

Uranus Angular: Dominating Independence = Outspoken

You are bold, daring, even reckless, and tend to shoot from the hip. You are highly original and free-thinking, and say whatever is on your mind. There can be a considerable no-nonsense bravado and self-superiority in your makeup, and a smug sense of humoring or tolerating other people. But you maintain your game high-spiritedness and optimism no matter what happens.

Uranus Cadent: Reactive Independence = Cagey

You tend to be cautious and conservative, and play your cards close to your chest. You are very aware of the opinion other people have of you, so you maintain a powerful governor on your impulses. You keep your own counsel, hedge your bets, and try not to make waves. Perhaps in compensation, you possess a keen intellectual detachment and a sardonic sense of humor.

Neptune Angular: Dominating Intuition = Certain
You have a bland nonchalance and willingness to act on your impulses and first impressions, and you unhesitatingly assume your rightful place in any social group. There may be something of Don Quixote about you: you are naïve, idealistic, and inclined to wander off in pursuit of your own visions and fancies. Since you rarely take counsel you may seem heedless at times, but you have an unshakeable faith in your own instincts which enables you to act with assurance and finality.

Neptune Cadent: Reactive Intuition = Worried
You are a bit apprehensive and self-justifying, and are tentative and lacking in inner certainty in your relations with other people. You are given to rumination, and you harbor doubts and second thoughts which hamper your spontaneity: you hedge, back-and-fill, and sidestep rather than confront. You can be rather suspicious, and have a tendency to see yourself as helpless or a victim. You may regard life as an onus or a heavy burden to be borne, but you usually volunteer to carry more than your share of the load.

Pluto Angular: Dominating Clarity = Uncompromising
You are quick to analyze possibilities, to make decisions, and then to charge right on ahead. You have an irrepressible spirit which licks its chops at conflict or opposition, and which always sticks to its guns. You succeed by refusing to back down and by immediately bouncing back from any defeat. Since you regard your own viewpoint as paramount you give little credence to others, but you are sure of the soundness and unassailability of your instincts and thinking.

Pluto Cadent: Reactive Clarity = Doubtful
You are a lone wolf who shies from scrutiny and sidesteps commitment. You don't stick your neck out by expressing your feelings, but rather try to manipulate matters from the background. You tend to put up with things rather than take direct action, and then you seethe and simmer and resent. You often feel helplessly buffeted about or taken advantage of. On your positive side you try to play the game by whatever you conceive the rules to be, and you have a spirit which is egalitarian and democratic.

Individual Planets conjunct Individual Angles

All of the angles symbolize strategies for controlling relationships. What is shown is a deftness in handling people, getting one's own way, getting other people's acceptance on one's own terms, bending other people to one's own will; these strategies are usually quite successful, which is why angularity is considered such a great strength. Natives with angular planets detach themselves from other people rather than allow themselves to be dragged along by others' caprices. Angularity produces a sense of fearlessness – or at least an insusceptibility to the doubts and second thoughts which hamper most people. Angular planet people need less validation and reassurance from others before they act.

All four angles show strategies for capitalizing (imposing your own rules) upon relationships, and the four angles symbolize four different types of relationships:

The Ascendant (Asc) symbolizes casual relationships;

The Descendant (Desc) symbolizes close relationships;

The Midheaven (MC) symbolizes group relationships; and

The Nadir (IC) symbolizes solitude.

That is, the Ascendant shows a way of facing people (of coming onto them); the Descendant shows a way of getting around, through, or past people; the Midheaven shows a way of dominating or directing people; and the Nadir shows a way of standing alone.

Planets conjunct the Ascendant symbolize a social ease, openness, candidness, straightforwardness – a way of laying all your cards on the table that cuts across the usual formalities and rituals which society imposes on casual relationships. These people have nothing to hide or apologize for, and nothing to fear or be ashamed of. They feel no need to ward other people off through such defenses as pride, irritation, brusqueness, preoccupation, etc. They are soft-spoken, yet firm and unyielding. They have a clear sense of personal space – their own and other peoples' – which is in no way puffed up or stiff. They are calm and relaxed, with no need to prove themselves or allow other people to impose upon them. People with rising planets succeed by disarming others; they make direct eye contact and are frank and outspoken without being offensive. They manifest an **intimacy** which is neither warm, compassionate, nor sweet, but is genuine nonetheless. They immediately put themselves on a personal basis with other people by being pleasant and inviting of manner, and by dealing with others on a basis of equality; and yet they are fundamentally cold – always maintaining their distance and reserve.

Planets conjunct the Descendant symbolize a species of psychological jujitsu – a way of winning people over by giving way to them. The action of a planet conjunct the Descendant is indirect; it reveals a basic stance or mood vis-à-vis other people rather than a superficial role being played. These planets let others take the lead overtly, directing the flow of things or pulling the strings from the background. Those with setting planets project a part of themselves onto other people, and get those other people to act out a role for them; therefore the action of a planet conjunct the Descendant can only be seen operating in close relationships, where propinquity and confinement make **manipulation** possible. After a fashion, setting planets do describe the marriage (or business) partner in the sense that they symbolize what natives seek in partnership – what part of themselves they want others to act out openly for them.

Planets conjunct the Midheaven show people controlling or taking the lead in a group, putting themselves in the saddle, pushing themselves onward and upward. Natives with these planets make a basic assumption of leadership or superiority (**dominance**): they possess a sense of special destiny and an urge to strike out on their own. Where those with rising planets know who they are, those with culminating planets know where they're going. They project a cool competence and expect to be looked up to and esteemed – role models for others to follow. Planets conjunct the Midheaven have a parental or mother-hen sense to them – responsible and protective, but also tending to herd other people around.

Planets conjunct the Nadir symbolize rootedness, conservatism, stability, staying power, **firmness**. Natives with these planets have an ability to remain unmoved and unruffled, to withstand the pressures of daily living by tuning into deeper currents or meanings in life. While all the angles symbolize a 'holding apart' from other people, the Nadir especially symbolizes going it alone. Planets conjunct this angle don't wait for others, rely on others, or depend on others. There is a spiritual manifestation with this angularity rather than a material one: from the spiritual point of view, the Nadir is actually the most powerful angle, since it is not as tied to the standards of success in society as are the other three angles – it shows a self-validating form of strength.

The following table gives key words for the various planets when angular. For example, the keyword for the Moon when conjunct any angle is **emotional**. Thus the Moon conjunct the Ascendant shows **emotional intimacy = tender**; the Moon conjunct the Descendant shows **emotional manipulation = stable**; the Moon conjunct the Midheaven shows **emotional dominance = protective**; and the Moon conjunct the Nadir shows **emotional firmness = intent**.

Interpretations for the Angular Planets

Sun/Asc – Sincere

You are down-to-earth, earnest, and plain-spoken. You have a sense of rightful place, and you are self-assured in any social situation and with people of all classes and stations. You fit yourself right in without being snobbish or pushy, which on the negative side can make you complacent and overreaching. You command respect by your sheer reasonableness and unruffled insouciance in any situation.

Sun/Desc – Influential

You are unassuming and solicitous, naturally reserved and formal, and don't permit people to get too close or too personal. You tend to stand behind a strong partner and pull the strings from the background. Because you are egalitarian and encouraging, others quite naturally defer to your authoritativeness and resolve.

Sun/MC – Utopian

You dedicate your life to a cause or belief system, and measure your progress against some abstract standard of morality and comportment, rather than in terms of social rewards. On the negative you can manifest an above-it-all superiority. But where most people are focused upon the path beneath their feet, you are always looking beyond the horizon towards an ideal reality.

Sun/IC – Staunch

Low-key and polite, you are also resolute, unyielding, and possess an unflagging perseverance and determination. On the negative side you

Keywords for the Angular Planets

		Ascendant:	Descendant:	Midheaven:	Nadir:
		Intimacy	Manipulation	Dominance	Firmness
Sun	Masterful	Sincere	Influential	Utopian	Staunch
Moon	Emotional	Tender	Stable	Protective	Intent
Mercury	Adroit	Fresh	Judicious	Glib	Canny
Venus	Childlike	Vulnerable	Game	Feisty	Gracious
Mars	Determined	Outfront	Steadfast	Gutsy	Assiduous
Jupiter	Philosophical	Benevolent	Avuncular	Perspicacious	Brisk
Saturn	Reserved	Cool	Uncompromising	Dignified	Modest
Uranus	Individualistic	Eccentric	Experimentative	Free-spirited	Doughty
Neptune	Private	Attuned	Removed	Retiring	Hopeful
Pluto	Potent	Flashy	Cunning	Competent	Stubborn
Ruler	Self-sufficient	Self-possessed	Self-contented	Self-sustaining	Self-cloistering

can be extremely obstinate and contrary, but other people can rely upon your integrity, scrupulousness, and deep sense of personal honor.

Moon/Asc – Tender
You are soft, gentle, and easily moved (wounded). You show your feelings quite openly – you wear your heart on your sleeve – which makes you a sympathetic listener on the one hand, but outspoken and tart on the other. Your subdued presence is calming and reassuring to others.

Moon/Desc – Stable
You are adaptable and improvisational, and you try your best to please and be pleasing. You are a supportive partner and let other people do their own thing, so you may attract partners who are moody and changeable. While you do hold to your guns when your principles are on the line (and then can be pigheaded and obdurate), most of the time you prefer to go with the flow, so other people find you real and relaxing to be with.

Moon/MC – Protective
You are at home in any group and like being sought after and looked up to. You possess a refinement and delicacy – on the negative side, prissiness – that is attuned to the psychological subtleties and the underlying feelings of other people in your social milieu. You try to include other people's points of view in your own thinking, and you project a sense of emotional equilibrium – of calm in the storm – to which others look for refuge.

Moon/IC – Intent
You are tenacious, persevering, and responsive primarily to your own inner voice. You have a pioneering spirit and you hearken to the beat of a distant drum, which on the negative side can make you solipsistic, stuffy, and stubborn. You are self-reliant and prefer being alone and on your own in life.

Mercury/Asc – Fresh
You are artless and guileless, and possess a youthful eagerness which takes delight in the simplest of things. You have a quixotic, irreverent good humor and a straightforwardness of manner which wins other people's confidence. Albeit a bit naïve and bumptious at times, your high spirits and cheerfulness provide the leavening in any group.

Mercury/Desc – Judicious

You are reasonable and conciliatory, and are willing to take other people's feelings and viewpoints into account in your own calculations. You possess a down-home simplicity and objectivity, which on the negative side can make you remote and noncommittal, and bring partners who make the decisions. You are believable and reasonable, and hence inspire the trust of others.

Mercury/MC – Glib

You are a good talker, offering a wry and perceptive commentary on the passing scene. You are unabashed, frank, and cocky – on the negative side, outspoken and brusque. You have a highly original point of view and slant on life, and you are the wellspring of good ideas and enthusiasm in any group.

Mercury/IC – Canny

You are cool-headed and high-principled, with keen powers of analysis. You play your cards close to your chest, and on the negative side can be suspicious and cynical of other people's motives. You are shrewd and emotionally guarded, with a great capacity for sober judgment and intellectual detachment in any emergency.

Venus/Asc – Vulnerable

You are genial, unaffected, and intimate. You have a simplicity of manner and knack for getting on a familiar basis with everyone you meet, which puts people immediately at their ease. Although you can be self-dramatizing and indulgent at times, you endear yourself to others with your unsophisticated impetuousness and optimism.

Venus/Desc – Game

You are plucky, experimentative, and willing to give other people's ideas and impulses a shot. You keep on an even emotional keel and actively seek peace and harmony, which at times can make you gullible or put-upon. People are swayed by your naïve enthusiasm and buoyancy even in the face of difficulties.

Venus/MC – Feisty

You are irreverent and possess a devil-may-care alacrity and bravado. You are positive and forward-looking, and say whatever is on your mind, which can make you peppery or swaggering. You are a good facilitator because you have a mischievous, elfin, saucy quality which seduces the acquiescence of others, making any activity enjoyable.

Venus/IC – Gracious
You are obliging, mannerly, and correct. You are meticulous and orderly, and are repelled by any harshness or indelicacy. On the negative side you can be overly punctilious and scrupulous, needing everything just so. You strive to create an agreeable and congenial environment and ambience for yourself and the people around you.

Mars/Asc – Outfront
You are unflinching and candid, and possess the ability to stand fast and hold your own in the face of adversity. Your placid, tractable exterior barely conceals a high-wire energy which is hardheaded, forceful, and domineering (on the negative side, contrary and deaf to reason). You are bold, blunt and never shy from expressing your opinions and making your presence be felt.

Mars/Desc – Steadfast
You are mild of manner, but also are headstrong, iron-willed, and something of a control freak in relationship. You are good-natured and obliging in the nonessentials, willing to give way when required, but never backing down from your basic position. You tend to attract partners who are as hardnosed as yourself. You have a knack for being forceful and unyielding without being overreaching or giving needless offense.

Mars/MC – Gutsy
You are fearless and adventurous, with considerable personal derring-do and panache. You are willing to take risks and to fly with your gut-level hunches, which at times can make for a pigheaded or absolutist streak. But you do have a knack for getting your own way by hook or crook, and always landing on your feet.

Mars/IC – Assiduous
You hold your feelings inside, keep a stiff upper lip, and cannot be diverted or deflected. You are cautious, thorough, and unrevealing, keeping your motives and plans to yourself. You have good powers of concentration and the ability to bring all your energy to bear upon your project or object of the moment.

Jupiter/Asc – Benevolent
You are hopeful and altruistic, with a good-natured bonhomie. You are not so much compassionate or sympathetic as humane, with a feeling of detached good will towards men. At times you can seem somewhat superior or a know-it-all. You prefer harmony and coexistence with other people, and take pains to respect their feelings and give them their due.

Jupiter/Desc – Avuncular
You have a detached goodwill and an accepting outlook on life and other people, and you tend to attract laid-back and accepting partners. You are concerned for others and do what you can to be helpful. Your cheerfulness even in suffering calls up the sympathy and good wishes of others in turn.

Jupiter/MC – Perspicacious
You are a model of equanimity, patience, and justice. You are able to take a long view, and so are undaunted by temporary setbacks, which can at times make you complacent and self-congratulatory. You are the backbone of any group because of your ironic good humor and ability to take difficulties in stride.

Jupiter/IC – Brisk
You are good-natured, tolerant, and resilient. You don't take things personally, but keep yourself remote and on a plane above it all – which can make you hard to reach or influence. Your smooth and lofty manner minimizes friction and bother, and keeps you free of compromising entanglements.

Saturn/Asc – Cool
You are composed, self-possessed, and outspoken (even curt), with an abstracted, brooding air. You have good analytical and critical faculties, and are most definite in your opinions. Your heavy, overbearing presence and sang-froid makes people fear you somewhat and keeps them at arm's length. You sway other people with your unvarnished frankness and unshakable conviction.

Saturn/Desc – Uncompromising
You are calm, level-headed, and serious, and tend to attract partners with whom you must go it alone. You are dogged and undaunted – on the negative side, intransigent – but you are always ready to shoulder

responsibility and go that extra mile. Your formidability awes and overwhelms other people.

Saturn/MC – Dignified

You have a strong sense of being anyone's equal, and of being able to hold your own come what may. You permit no trespass upon your private space, and you endeavor not to depend too much upon others, which gives you a strong need to be in absolute control. You are at your best when working by and for yourself.

Saturn/IC – Modest

You are plain, unvarnished, and unpretentious (undiplomatic). You are neither timid nor shy, but rather are unobtrusive – a simple person with simple needs. You hide nothing, defend nothing, and keep your distance by being wide-open and nonjudgmental.

Uranus/Asc – Eccentric

You are truly an original, with a unique and unusual point of view, and an unabashed indifference to what other people think of you. You can be a tough cookie to tangle with: ornery, determined, and headstrong. Although you have a flamboyant personality and let it all hang out, you aren't pushy but are inclined to give others as much space as you demand for yourself.

Uranus/Desc – Experimentative

You are forthright, self-sufficient, and impulsive, and you tend to attract partners of strong character and willpower as well. Although you can be fancy-free to the point of capriciousness and wrong-headedness, your imagination, boldness, and irrepressibility create a momentum which sweeps other people up and carries them along.

Uranus/MC – Free-Spirited

You are idealistic and visionary – truly an original – and recognize no authority but your own. Your bravado can be charming in its proper moment but also overweening or contumacious at its worst. You are perceptive and intellectually quick. You prefer to strike out on your own rather than conform to society's expectations of you.

Uranus/IC – Doughty

You are dynamic, resourceful, and free-thinking (on the negative side, oblivious). You have a capacity for plunging ahead and making sudden, drastic changes in your environment and life-style whenever your life situation becomes too restrictive.

Neptune/Asc – Attuned

You have a great capacity for understanding the feelings of others. You are able to pick up and address emotional undercurrents – what's really going on beneath the surface – in any relationship. You have a dark, preoccupied, abstracted air: you are on your own wavelength – not so much spaced-out as brooding and introspective.

Neptune/Desc – Removed

You are genial and pleasant outwardly, but basically you are secretive, uncommunicative, and keep your own counsel – and you tend to attract partners who are not altogether there either. You are neither selfish nor reclusive, but rather trust completely in your own instincts, and thus have little need for the reassurance of others.

Neptune/MC – Retiring

You follow the dictates of your own heart rather than worry about living up to other people's images, and as a result can be brusque and unmannerly at times. Albeit outwardly sociable, this is just a mask you wear to fulfill other people's expectations so that they'll leave you alone to follow your own dream. You lack worldly ambition since your chief desire is for an island of peace unto yourself away from the world's clamor.

Neptune/IC – Hopeful

You tend to be upright, principled, and high-minded, with a tendency to withdraw into yourself or into nature. You have a quixotic idealism and a positive approach to life which looks to the good sides of people and events without being naïve or easily gulled.

Pluto/Asc – Flashy

You come on strong and make a powerful impression, though you have the saving grace of an ironic good-humor. You are alert and opportunistic, driven by a high-wire energy, and at times you bowl people right over. Your do your own thing with considerable personal flair and dash.

Pluto/Desc – Cunning

You are outspoken and to the point, even a bit sarcastic or sassy, and have a gift for seeing clearly through superficial role-playing and posturing.

You can be rather calculating and manipulative, and you attract exacting partners as a result. You are able to avoid other people's snares because you are alert to their covert manipulations, and you are not afraid to call a spade a spade.

Pluto/MC – Competent
You are confident, thoroughgoing, and decisive, and you believe that you are capable of anything, which on the negative side can make you snobbish or stand-off-ish. Together with your can-do optimism you are scrupulous, meticulous, and willing to go to any extreme to implement your vision.

Pluto/IC – Stubborn
You are self-assured and opinionated, and you are capable of taking a position and making a stand without being arrogant or offensive. You are overtly agreeable and tractable, and you are skilled in the art of winning acquiescence without yielding an inch.

Ruler Asc conjunct Asc – Self-Possessed
You are straightforward and direct, and mince no words (tactless). You are able to be yourself – natural and at ease – in any surroundings. You are proud, stately, and never compromise your dignity.

Ruler Desc conjunct Desc – Self-Contented
You are breezy, insouciant, and unaffected (self-centered). You are confident and have a positive outlook because you feel complete unto yourself. You don't need (or leave much room for) the support of other people in your life.

Ruler MC conjunct MC – Self-Sustaining
You have an unflagging faith in yourself and your ability to succeed (overweening). You are never at a loss, but are able to make the best of whatever situation you find yourself in.

Ruler IC conjunct IC – Self-Cloistering
You are friendly and sociable, but fundamentally are a loner, and you find sustained contact with other people grating or enervating (self-pampering). You are happiest and do your best work alone, on your own.

3

Aspectual State

Where terrestrial strength refers to success in social role-playing, aspectual strength refers to ease or effort in the native's adaptation to his or her immediate environment. Everyone has certain prototypal personal experiences and relationships just by virtue of their being human: infancy – childhood – play – schooling – adolescence – sexual awakening – marriage – parenting – work – participation in religious and social activities. These are what individual aspects refer to. For example, Sun-Mercury and Sun-Venus (taken together) refer to the Inner Child (and the native's relationship with the parent); Moon-Venus and Sun-Mars aspects refer to the Anima and Animus – the female and male sides of the native's personality (and, by extension, relationships with women or men in general); Venus-Mars aspects refer to relationships with the opposite sex, and so forth.

The aspects in a chart reveal what is normally considered good or bad luck in everyday life relationships and situations: well-aspected charts indicate an easy adjustment to – and good luck in – everyday life; afflicted charts indicate the contrary. Aspectual strength doesn't measure success as angularity does, but rather the basic take on life: cooperation/comfort versus sacrifice/struggle. People who seem to be able to get things to click for them with no sweat have charts which are largely well-aspected, while people for whom things only come by blood, sweat and tears – and not even then much of the time – have afflicted charts. But this is not the same thing as success in the world: charts with lots of angular planets will tend to be more successful (get what they want) than charts without angular planets, no matter what is going on with respect to the aspects, which indicate only how success (or failure) comes – easily, or with difficulty.

Everybody is in pain – *everybody* is suffering. That's just life, as the Buddhists say. Natives with well-aspected charts are in no less pain than natives with afflicted charts. However they've learned better pain management. They don't allow their pain to obsess them – they relax into it instead of clenching up against it. Ergo, they can relax into pleasure as well. Afflicted chart natives bear their pain openly. They have an itchy, picky impatience with themselves and other people. They confront their pain directly – keep pinching themselves – instead of masking it or passing over it. They hug it to their bosoms, deferring their pleasure indefinitely.

The difference between well-aspected and afflicted-chart natives is that the former live strategically, go with the flow, and as a result people tend to accept them on their own terms, whereas the latter stumble and bumble and struggle against the flow, and as a result they tend to be rejected by people. Well-aspected actions are **detached**, whereas afflicted actions are **maladjusted**. Well-aspected chart natives avoid getting involved in other people's karma, whereas afflicted-chart natives actively seek to mirror their own inner turmoil by projecting it outward in relationships and circumstances. Well-aspected chart natives are loose and easy, whereas afflicted-chart natives are tense and tight. Well-aspected chart natives take things in stride, whereas afflicted-chart natives take things personally and are easily affronted. Well-aspected chart natives let go, whereas afflicted-chart natives cling and cling.

As might be expected, well-aspected planets and charts are better for material matters, and afflicted planets and charts are better for spiritual matters. Natives with well-aspected charts have the ability to make the best of things and not get into too much of an uproar, but they also tend to be complacent, self-satisfied, and spiritually lazy. By contrast, natives with afflicted charts are intense, blustery, jarring, and at war with themselves and their environment, but their discontent is a powerful motive force towards the development of true detachment and wisdom.

So, in the case of the well-aspected/afflicted distinction, what is being measured is how well the natives get things to come through for them with a minimum of fuss. A well-aspected chart is not usually good for meticulousness, thoroughness, endurance, steadfastness, etc. unless there are strong testimonies to the contrary, such as a powerful Saturn, or a stellium or preponderance of planets in earth signs. Natives with well-aspected horoscopes are more apt to walk away from serious difficulties or compromising entanglements; indeed, they will rarely draw these sorts of circumstances to themselves in the first place, since they don't enter into relationships or situations which they cannot control. On the other hand, afflicted charts are not usually good for things like calm, reasoned decision or disinterested objectivity. These natives are scrappers, who are always impelled to choose sides (often the losing ones). As Charles Carter says in *The Astrological Aspects*, "It stands to reason that, since to achieve anything notable is *ex hypothesi* difficult, the map of the man who does this must contain difficult elements."[1]

Even when they are strong by celestial and terrestrial state, afflicted charts indicate frustration, obstacles, unfulfilled expectations; anticipated rewards for expended effort are not forthcoming. These natives are unable to fit in or get others to cooperate, thus peoples' afflicted planets show how and why other people reject them.

As an example, my own horoscope is quite strong by celestial state (the Sun is sole dispositor), and my chart is also quite strong by terrestrial state (with 5 planets – including the Sun – angular). And, in fact, I've gotten to do pretty much as I pleased in life: I determined the basic lineaments of my life and the course it would take; I answered to no one but my own conscience, and I made my own decisions for myself. I have also managed to make all of my important dreams come true: I live a leisurely life in a tropical paradise and have made some amazing spiritual connections here; most days I wake up in the morning when I naturally wake up, and then I decide what I feel like doing that day; I have servants to do my house work and gardening; I don't have to take responsibility for anyone but myself, moreover, I am well on the way to realizing my lifelong spiritual and artistic goals. However, in spite of its favorable celestial and terrestrial states, my horoscope is badly afflicted: my family, marriage, and all other attempts at intimate relationships (apart from friendships) have been utterly disastrous; every business I've started has crashed; for most of my adult life I have been on a tight money choke-chain, and until recently, it's been an uphill struggle every step of the way. In other words, my horoscope's favorable celestial and terrestrial states indicate that I've always kept the faith; believed in myself, and have pretty much gotten to do my own thing (once I reached adulthood). But my horoscope's afflicted aspectual state means

---

1. Charles Carter, *The Astrological Aspects*, Fowler, London, 1971, page 12.

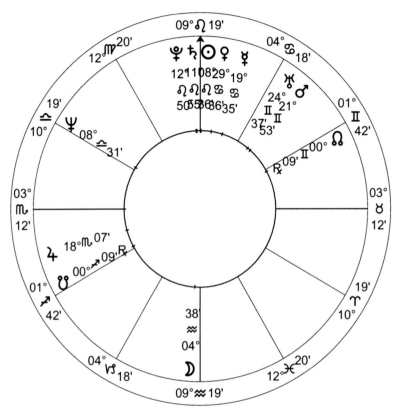

Bob Makransky: 1 August 1947, 01.09.50 pm EDT, Philadelphia, PA, USA.

that it's also been a lot of slings and arrows of outrageous fortune (not that my own hubris was not a contributing factor).

In short, where celestial and terrestrial strength refer to inner states (satisfaction and adroitness, respectively), aspectual strength refers to interaction with the outer world: whether a planet operates smoothly and efficiently, or only with great effort and expenditure. Where terrestrial strength refers to success in social relationships, aspectual strength refers to success in personal relationships (whether the native is accepted or rejected by others and by the vicissitudes of circumstances). This is why unaspected planets are actually 'stronger' than even well-aspected planets, since they sidestep the issues of success versus failure, winning versus losing, and acceptance versus rejection. The meaning of an unaspected planet is similar in meaning to that of the planet conjunct the Ascendant, and is also about of the same strength: forthright, unhesitating, gut-level, self-expression. Unaspected planets are relatively detached, and therefore they will be discussed separately at the end of this chapter (which for heuristic reasons emphasizes the well-aspected versus afflicted polarity).

> "First: with their aspects benefic planets confer good things. Clearly they do so easily and amply with good aspects if the planet is well disposed and in a good House of the figure; but with the bad aspects, (they confer good) only with difficulty." [Morinus Book 18, page 63].

Well-aspected planets (and charts) tend to get things to click for them, whereas afflicted planets (and charts) stumble over every pebble, they balk at every mischance and take the things that happen very personally rather than shrug them off philosophically. Whether this mindset attracts difficult circumstances or whether difficult circumstances condition a negative mindset is moot. The point is that afflicted charts make for Hard-Luck Harrys. In other words, of the three principal types of strength – celestial, terrestrial, and aspectual – aspectual strength is most closely indicative of what is commonly referred to as 'luck' – getting the outside world and other people to cooperate.

Aspects cannot really be looked at in isolation but must be considered in terms of the greater configurations to which they belong: it is not enough to sum up the number of harmonious and disharmonious aspects (within given orbs) to a planet in order to determine its aspectual strength. Rather, each planet must be viewed in terms of any configurations in which it participates to evaluate whether that planet is well-aspected, afflicted, or a mixture (successful and capable in some types of situations and relationships, self-defeating in others). In particular, the short leg of a T-cross can be considered to be seriously afflicted, and the mediating planet of a wedge can be considered to be quite well-aspected indeed.

For example, in my own chart Neptune is quite well-aspected since it is the point planet of a wedge mediating an opposition between Moon and Sun-Saturn-Pluto, and indeed psychedelic drug and plant experiences have always been most beneficial to my spiritual growth and happiness. Moreover, I continually receive valuable guidance and information talking to spirits and trees. On the other hand, Jupiter (ruler of the 2nd house) in my chart is rather afflicted since it is the short leg of a wide T-cross involving that same opposition, and money has always been my bete noire (having south node in the 2nd house doesn't help much either). Contrariwise, I've noticed that people with an afflicted Neptune probably shouldn't mess around with drugs, and they tend to get involved with the wrong sorts of spirits; money tends to flow easily to people with a well-aspected Jupiter.

Consider too that conjunction with the Moon's North Node must be reckoned as a powerful harmonious aspect, and conjunction with the South Node a serious affliction. Also, obviously a trine by Jupiter is more favorable than one by Saturn and a square by Mars is more unfavorable than one by Venus. Also, conjunction with Jupiter isn't all that terrible even for the planets it combines with disharmoniously. On the other hand, conjunction with Saturn usually damages a planet more than Saturn is damaged by it; similarly, Mercury and Venus are more afflicted by conjunction with the Sun than the Sun is afflicted by conjunction with Mercury or Venus. Also, the question of harmony/disharmony is relative: Sun conjunct Mars (headstrong, self-certain, adamant) is good for the native, but perhaps not so great for people who have to deal with that native. Also, aspects involving a planet's dispositor (ruler of the sign in which it is posited) become more important by that fact alone.

As Morinus points out, "An aspect between two planets is to be considered in terms of the supremacy of one of the planets over the other, for when two planets are conjunct, square, or in opposition, and the question arises as to which will be the more powerful, the answer will be found by a consideration of four points:

1)   The dignity of the planets in aspect for – other things being equal – the Sun and Moon supersede the other planets in importance because they are the principal bodies over the earth, and of these the Sun supersedes the Moon. Furthermore the superior planets Saturn, Jupiter and Mars are more powerful than the inferior ones Venus and Mercury....

2)   The celestial state, for the planet stronger by celestial state – that is, by domicile, exaltation, triplicity, and position with respect to the Sun, etc. – wins out over the planet which is weaker.

3)   The terrestrial state, for that one of the aspecting planets which through its local determinations influences for good or for ill the affairs of the houses into which the aspects fall will prevail.

4)   Application and separation, for a planet which applies to another planet by aspect is said to be the stronger of the two."[2] [Morinus Book 21, pages 86-7].

In other words, there's no simple way of defining what is meant by 'well-aspected' versus 'afflicted' in general. There are too many factors which must be taken into account, and any weighting system is going to be most arbitrary. Thus we are forced to employ the terms 'well-aspected' and 'afflicted' without being able to specify precisely what these terms actually mean.

The most harmonious configurations are *grand trines* (120°-120°-120°), *grand sextiles* (60°-60°-60°-60°-60°-60°), and *fans* (120°-60°-60°).

Generally harmonious configurations, composed of oppositions festooned with sextiles and trines, include *5/6th*, *kites* (120°-60°-60°-120°), *rectangles* (120°-60°-120°-60°), *trapezoids* (180°-60°-60°-60°), and *wedges* (180°-120°-60°). Albeit nominally disharmonious, the opposition cannot be said to be necessarily bad. Where the conjunction indicates self-adequacy, the opposition indicates a striving (for some sort of balance or quid pro quo from other people), but this can be a matter of collaboration as much as conflict. It depends on whether the planets involved combine harmoniously or disharmoniously, thus the *Table of Favorable and Unfavorable Planetary Combinations* below applies as well to oppositions as to conjunctions. And, as Morinus would say, it also depends upon whether the planets involved are weak or strong by celestial state (we shall examine this point in the following chapter).

Indeed, neither conjunctions nor oppositions can be considered innately harmonious or disharmonious. Dr. Marc Edmund Jones considered the absence of oppositions in a horoscope to be a definite

---

2. "Finally, we must here point out that applying planetary conjunctions and aspects are more powerful than separating ones. Also, sinister aspects are more forceful than dexter ones." [Morinus Book 18, page 63]. As with the oriental/occidental distinction (to be discussed later on), I personally find that applying aspects have a different flavor than separating ones do – i.e. that this is not a strength factor per se. Similarly for dexter (waxing) and sinister (waning) aspects.

handicap in the life of a native, and Morinus considers that "an entirely fortunate planet causes good by its opposition." [Morinus Book 18, page 64].

Oppositions are aspects of self-awareness: a lack of oppositions implies a lack of inner conflict, but also a lack of objectivity and self-perspective. There is no way that natives lacking in oppositions can ever see things from the other fellow's point of view. Like horses with blinders, their vision is limited to the path beneath their feet. And since (as Chogyam Trungpa put it) a sense of humor means seeing both poles of a situation as they are, from an aerial point of view, natives lacking oppositions also tend to lack a real sense of humor. They can laugh *at*, but not *with*. Natives lacking oppositions shy away from commitment and contention (i.e. opposition) and prefer not to confront other people – and life – directly.

Nonetheless, even when the planets involved combine favorably, configurations involving squares tend to be difficult, involving constant crises, turmoil, conflict, or disappointment. The disharmonious configurations are *grand squares* (90°-90°-90°-90°) and *T-crosses* (90°-180°-90°).

Conjunction charts such as *stelliums* (mass conjunctions involving four or more planets, signifying heaviness, focus, concentration, tenacity, dedication, single-mindedness and immovability), and also charts which contain *close pairs* (where the planets tend to aggregate in conjunctions around the chart, signifying cleverness, versatility, resourcefulness, improvisation, and the ability to land on one's feet), can be either favorable or unfavorable, depending upon whether the planets involved (particularly adjacent planets in a stellium) are intrinsically harmonious or disharmonious with each other (see the *Table of Favorable and Unfavorable Planetary Combinations* below); also upon their dignities (how weak or strong by sign the individual planets are, and how near they are to angles).

It is customary to take wider orbs of inexactitude in considering configurations than is done in considering individual aspects. Here, we arbitrarily allow 6° orbs of inexactitude when we are considering an aspect in isolation (e.g. in defining 'unaspected'), but much larger orbs can be taken when considering a configuration. Just having three planets in the three different signs of the same element (fire – earth – air – water) confers much of the virtue of a grand trine, even when the individual trine aspects are way out of orb. Similarly, four planets in the four signs of the same quadruplicity (cardinal – fixed – mutable) operate much like a grand square even when the individual aspects are over orb.

When there are both harmonious and disharmonious configurations in the same horoscope, then in some areas of the native's life (shown by the symbolism of the relevant planets and houses) the native's life will be harmonious, and in others, disharmonious.

Preponderance of well-aspected planets (6 or more): you are natural, at ease, and inclined to take things as they come. You live in a world of your own, and don't permit yourself to become too personally involved or committed. You keep loose, aloof, circumspect. You are practical and down-to-earth, and operate smoothly and effectively.

Preponderance of afflicted planets (6 or more): you are headstrong, proud, and unyielding. You tend to be a bit vain or possess an air of smug superiority, and you tend to be headstrong, pugnacious, and heavy-handed in dealing with others. You often feel beset on all sides, rather easily become frazzled or harassed, and you rely upon dogged obduracy to see you through.

Keywords for Aspectual State of Planets

Planet	Strengthens/ Weakens	Well- aspected	Afflicted	Unaspected
		Detached	Maladjusted	Singular
Sun	Purpose	Aloof	Resistant	Positive
Moon	Assurance	Blithe	Moody	Mindful
Mercury	Mentality	Nimble	Dogmatic	Candid
Venus	Enjoyment	Perky	Broody	Genial
Mars	Accomplishment	Efficient	Ornery	Pert
Jupiter	Understanding	Ingenuous	Contrary	Composed
Saturn	Responsibility	Ready	Bull-Headed	Tenacious
Uranus	Independence	Hearty	Rebellious	Uninhibited
Neptune	Intuition	Trusting	Wary	Deliberate
Pluto	Clarity	Apropos	Obsessive	Observant

Interpretations for Aspectual State

Sun Well-aspected: Detached Purpose = Aloof

While by no means self-effacing, you prefer not to vaunt yourself but rather to let your actions speak for themselves. You get things to click for you by keeping your cool – by being low-key and conciliatory, and not fruitlessly battering your head against walls. You inspire trust because you are high-principled, straightforward, and you make the assumption of good faith and integrity in all your doings.

Sun Afflicted: Maladjusted Purpose = Resistant

You have something of a struggle ethic – a drive to be constantly proving or vindicating yourself – and you waste a lot of energy in posturing and making your point, perhaps due to a harsh, critical, or unsuccessful father against whom you measure yourself. Because you deliberately take the path less traveled you are constantly forced to defend yourself, to alter your expectations and outlook, to modify your goals and ambitions. Even when you are successful you feel as though you are on an endless treadmill. But you are resilient and feisty, and are able to pop right back up again whenever your dreams crash.

Moon Well-aspected: Detached Assurance = Blithe

You are optimistic, and hopeful – always looking on the bright side and expecting the best. You have a fresh, buoyant, childlike spirit, and you follow your fancy wherever it may lead you. On the other hand, you can be unduly carefree, gaily sloughing off relationship issues or other pressing responsibilities, no matter how exigent they may be. You maintain an unruffled air and keep your composure no matter what is going on around you.

Moon Afflicted: Maladjusted Assurance = Moody

You are fiercely proud, defiant, and quick to resent a slight. Often due to early conflicts or abandonment issues with your mother, you do not know the art of yielding gracefully, but rather nurse your wounds whenever you feel you're being pressured or compelled. This gives you a dark, sullen side which unnerves people and inclines them to keep their distance; you confront issues by closing up into yourself and keeping your own counsel. On the other hand, your well-meaning honesty compels the respect of others.

Mercury Well-aspected: Detached Mentality = Nimble

You are adroit, shrewd, and have a positive and saucy optimism which people find entertaining. You possess a fresh and somewhat impudent way of looking at things, so your conversation is lively and people are happy to listen to you. On the other hand, you possess a rather smug, know-it-all attitude which – albeit charming and amusing in its proper moment – can also become overweening or overbearing. But your ability to see past conventional mores and taken-for-granted assumptions inspires fresh thinking and problem-solving in other people.

Mercury Afflicted: Maladjusted Mentality = Dogmatic

You have a tendency towards circular thinking, getting stuck in the same mental ruts and repeating the same internal monologue, over and over and over again. It is difficult for you to take a long view since your current circumstances tend to be in continual crises. You rely upon stubbornness and obstinate single-mindedness to get your way; you wear people down rather than win them over, but your seriousness, tenacity, and willingness to go it alone get you through any difficulty.

Venus Well-aspected: Detached Enjoyment = Perky

You are outgoing and ingratiating, and take a genuine interest in your fellows. Your personal manner is breezy, cool, and efficient, and you have a positive, cheerful outlook on life. There is a sense of personal style, flair, or craftsmanship in all that you do. You seek harmony and sidestep conflict whenever possible. You tend to take things in your stride and not permit yourself to be disconcerted by events, which on the negative side can mean putting up with unacceptable people or situations. You try to maintain a pleasant exterior and remain open to what is happening.

Venus Afflicted: Maladjusted Enjoyment = Broody

You tend to be simplistic and naïve in your dealings with people, and are inclined to play the uncomprehending victim being pushed around by circumstances. You are overly intent upon the path beneath your feet and thus miss out on many of life's little opportunities and surprises. You are can be super-sensitive, pugnacious, and suspicious of people's motives rather than open to their gestures. Of necessity you learn how to shake off discouragement and rejection, and stand on your own two feet.

Mars Well-aspected: Detached Accomplishment = Efficient
You are cool and capable, and go about your business without much fuss or pother. You have an outgoing, mischievous personality and a keen analytical mind, and you are daring, unique, and original. You know how to wheedle other people to get your own way with them, but when you can't you go off on your own without a fare-thee-well. Although you know how to take a stand, and cannot be deflected when once you have made up your mind, you don't let yourself get into an uproar but maintain your distance and your dignified reserve.

Mars Afflicted: Maladjusted Accomplishment = Ornery
You are independent-minded and scrappy, and are quick to resent and to tangle. Although you do possess an idiosyncratic nobility of spirit – or at least a steadfast refusal to compromise your principles – other people tend find you contentious and wrong-headed: you call a spade a spade, and your personal manner can be quite indelicate and jarring. You often feel put upon or buffeted about, and you dig in your heels and depend upon stonewalling people in order to maintain control. On the positive side you are self-sufficient, resourceful, and never say die.

Jupiter Well-aspected: Detached Understanding = Ingenuous
You have a friendly, open, welcoming manner and are a good listener. There is a simplicity and candor about you which puts people at their ease, so others tend to accept you on your own terms. You are earnest and straightforward in your speech and broad in your outlook, and you have a detached, philosophical, live-and-let-live point of view. Your air of impartial disinterest and sympathetic concern inspires the confidence and trust of others. You win support with your own unvarnished enthusiasm and jaunty *joie de vivre*.

Jupiter Afflicted: Maladjusted Understanding = Contrary
Your approach to other people is tentative and unsure: you may try a little too hard, are a little too pushy and insistent, or else you close up and turn a deaf ear to others. Because you are out of synch with where other people are coming from and don't rightly gauge their reactions and limits, you may overstep yourself or grate on people. Other people find you a bit overweening or presumptuous, with a prima donna self-dramatization and a tendency to convince by fait accompli. But you

maintain your quixotic optimism and noble steadfastness no matter what happens.

Saturn Well-aspected: Detached Responsibility = Ready

You are optimistic, cheerful, and forward-looking, with a love of challenge and novelty. You are able to hold your own and follow your own star without giving needless offense. You are impersonal, impervious, and maintain a polite distance between yourself and other people. You keep on an even keel and try not to make waves, you don't believe in taking life or other people too seriously. Although you are cool and condescending, and can seem overly unreachable at times, nonetheless you are wholehearted and venturesome, and are determined to enjoy yourself come what may.

Saturn Afflicted: Maladjusted Responsibility = Bull-Headed

You are contentious, self-exculpating, and always at pains to make your point or get in the last word. Overly sensitive and peppery, you easily feel victimized or put out by circumstances; and you bridle at authority and direction. You either brazen it out or else charge right on ahead and damn the torpedoes, and although you may try to appeal to other peoples' reason, you can be remarkably obtuse and insensitive to their perceptions and points of view. Albeit easily bogged down in details and side issues, you stick to your guns come hell or high water.

Uranus Well-aspected: Detached Independence = Hearty

You are free-spirited and gritty, and you go your own way and do your own thing with nary a by-your-leave. You are not so much loutish as slippery; good at dodging commitment and compromise, hard to pin down, and you sidestep collisions and confrontations whenever possible. Yet you are by no means a shrinking violet: you have sharp lines which are not to be crossed, and when once you have made a stand, there is no one more stubborn and unflinching. You have a positive, can-do attitude and are a model of staunch independence of spirit to all who know you.

Uranus Afflicted: Maladjusted Independence = Rebellious

Although you are very idealistic and do follow your own impulses with unquestioning faith (which can be rather charming in its place), your naive self-assurance often strikes other people as being bumptious, pushy, and bruising. You have a tendency to bristle under the slightest restraint and to run roughshod over other people's sensibilities. You operate with a sense of incumbency or strain, as if you need to be constantly proving yourself or testing your mettle. You are earnest and well-meaning, and your strong sense of honor wins the respect of others.

Neptune Well-aspected: Detached Intuition = Trusting

You are high-minded, idealistic and always willing to follow your own vision wherever it may lead you. You may have an artistic or creative bent, and you brim with a naive enthusiasm and *joie de vivre*. You are a dreamer, with your head in the clouds, and may possess considerable psychic ability. You are straightforward and transparent in your own motives, and you thus inspire the trust and confidence of other people.

Neptune Afflicted: Maladjusted Intuition = Wary

(Note: Everyone born since the mid-1940s has Neptune sextile Pluto, so there's going to be a limit as to how afflicted either of these planets can be). You are often off on your own wavelength and out of touch with what other people consider to be the realities of the situation. You tend to distrust or eschew the common wisdom and are suspicious of other people's motives, so people can find you overly guarded, closed-minded, and deaf to reason. But you are staunchly single-minded and intent, and you follow your gut-level impulses all the way to the end.

Pluto Well-aspected: Detached Clarity = Apropos

You have a unique ability to rise to any occasion and be equal to any event. You are plucky, shrewd, and knowing, and can see quite clearly into the hidden motives of other people. You can draw upon considerable personal charm in order to finesse and get your way with people – you have a winning attitude and a pioneering spirit which blazes new trails for others to follow. Your vibrant energy and positive outlook inspire the people around you.

Pluto Afflicted: Maladjusted Clarity = Obsessive

You are quick to feel embattled and at war, which gives you an absolutist or dictatorial streak. You often feel misunderstood or obstructed, and you can be quite thorny to deal with – unreasonable or wrong-headed – when simple compromise would suffice. Your life is punctuated now and then by 180° reversals, or by complete wipe-outs in which you must start your life over again from zero. Although you tend to butt your way through things, you nonetheless possess an admirable courage, tenacity, and persistence.

Table of Favorable and Unfavorable Planetary Combinations (per Morinus)

	SU	MO	ME	VE	MA	JU
MO	+					
ME	+	+				
VE	+	+	+			
MA	+	−	−	−		
JU	+	+	+	+	−	
SA	−	−	+	−	−	+

Table of Favorable and Unfavorable Planetary Combinations (per Makransky)

	SU	MO	ME	VE	MA	JU	SA	UR	NE
MO	+								
ME	−	+							
VE	−	+	−						
MA	+	−	+	+					
JU	+	+	−	+	+				
SA	−	−	+	−	−	+			
UR	+	−	+	−	+	+	+		
NE	−	+	−	+	−	+	−	+	
PL	+	−	+	−	+	−	−	−	−

Unaspected Planets

> "If a strong planet has no aspect with another planet it is said to be feral and will act simply in accordance with its own nature, especially if located in its domicile. Every feral planet indicates something unusual – good or ill – depending on the nature of the planet; for example, Saturn feral in the first indicates the hermit or monk." [Morinus Book 21, page 91].

It's a general rule of thumb in astrology that nothing is better than something. For example, it's best for the affairs symbolized by a given house in the natal horoscope if there are no planets in that house. Even benefic planets well-aspected in a house cause complications, excesses (if not conflicts), etc., whereas an empty house is quiescent. It may not bring opportunities, but neither does it bring problems.

In the same way it's better for a natal planet to be unaspected than for it to participate in even benefic aspects. This is because the principle represented by that planet is then at its freest; a lack of aspects symbolizes the purest expression of a planetary energy, untainted by any admixture of doubt, ulterior motive, or conscious purpose and design.

All of the aspects – whether harmonious or disharmonious – symbolize ways of hooking up to society's wheel of rewards and punishments. An aspect symbolizes some kind of sweat or stew, some area of concern, something to be grasped or avoided, some point to be made or defended – in short, something pending in the life: some part of the personality which is not at peace within itself.

The parallels of declination at least direct the combination of planetary energies towards some species of self-validation, but the zodiacal aspects direct it towards seeking, seeking, seeking, something or someone 'out there' to fill in whatever piece of the self seems to be missing.

By contrast, unaspected planets are solitary wanderers. They are more directly attuned to the Spirit – are less influenced by society's static – than are the aspected planets. It is not so much a question of self-validation (which is symbolized by the parallels) as it is a true detachment from and indifference to social sanctions and rewards. The unaspected planet, therefore, is the social performer par excellence, because it doesn't have to solicit some stock reaction from other people (as aspected planets do).

In the part of their personalities ruled by their unaspected planet(s), natives are truly relaxed with other people since they do not submit themselves to others for approval or rejection of their acts, and therefore people are able to relax with them in turn. The unaspected planet in a chart is like the eye of a hurricane – a place of repose and tranquility in the midst of a hurried, agitated rush.

Natives' unaspected planets show how and where in life they are free from other people's – and society's – pushing and tugging at them. Natives who lack unaspected planets have no such refuge (point of contact with the outside world in a spirit of harmony and peace). To have every planet in aspect is to be completely caught up in society's game plan of success or failure, acceptance or rejection, power or powerlessness, glory or shame, etc. It means that there is no natural respite from the necessity of impressing people, hiding from people, faking it with people, etc.

By contrast, the unaspected planet in a horoscope (and with 6° orbs for the Ptolemaic aspects – conjunction, sextile, square, trine, and opposition – roughly half of all charts will possess at least one unaspected planet) symbolizes a light and delicate touch with others instead of a tug to jerk them and oneself about. The reason why the unaspected planet is unmoved by worldly glory is because it symbolizes a profound isolation, cosmic anguish, which comes across to others as a feeling of sadness.

We can say that all of the aspects (except for the parallel) symbolize some form or another of self-pity. The unaspected planet does not dull the feeling of cosmic anguish – separatedness – with self-pity, but rather feels it directly as sadness. The sadness of the unaspected planet is not a protection or a defense against hurt; it doesn't withdraw into itself as a tactic of avoidance. Rather, it is a symbol of the true understanding that we are alone in this life, and that any assumption to the contrary is an illusion.

Because it feels itself to be isolated and vulnerable (but in no sense helpless), the unaspected planet exhibits a reverence and gentleness with life and other people which the aspects tend to take for granted or overlook in their machinations and manipulations. The unaspected planet has a strong sense of personal space – its own, and that of other people. It knows how not to overstep itself, not intrude itself upon others, nor presume too much.

The unaspected planet is operating at that planet's highest potential. The planetary energy is neither impeded (as it is by disharmonious aspects) nor biased (as it is by harmonious aspects), but is in its freest and most creative state of being. Thus a lack of aspects must be considered to be the greatest benefic aspect of all.

Preponderance of Unaspected Planets (three or more using 6° orbs)
You possess a great personal dignity and integrity – a directness, simplicity, and lack of guile which is the outward hallmark of self-acceptance and inner peace. Albeit stubborn and determined when your principles are on the line, you are not out to prove or defend yourself, and you greet life with a feeling of openness and live-and-let-live toleration. You are isolated from others, cut off from their rat race of eagerness and turmoil, without being callous or closed-hearted to them. On the contrary you are respectful, tender, and mild. You have a sense of *Angst* and the pain of the human condition which is in no way morbid or self-pitying, but rather is optimistic, hopeful, and encouraging to others. Your wisdom and compassion are a refuge and support for other people.

Sun Unaspected – Positive
You have a truly sunny disposition, a magnanimous and inviting manner, and a positive outlook on yourself and other people. You make direct eye contact, and you have a pixie-like twinkle which disarms people and puts them at their ease. Albeit democratic and egalitarian in your approach to others, you possess a great personal pride, a noble bearing, and a regal self-assurance born of a true sense of divine right (touch with the Spirit). Your pride is not a superiority to other people based upon comparing yourself to them, but rather is a sure knowledge that inside yourself there is good, and that all is as it should be in the world. You don't hold yourself apart from others, you just *are* apart from them, on a solitary track in life. Thus you are able to immediately put yourself on a personal basis with everyone you meet without entangling yourself in their webs of self-importance. It's not that you are so humble (you're not), but rather that at the deepest strata of your being you have made your peace with the universe. Without trying, intending, or even caring for the role, you find that other people quite naturally look up to you as a paradigm of right attitude and comportment.

Moon Unaspected – Mindful

Although you are sociable, gregarious, and voluble, the social and interactive part of you is but the tip of an iceberg. In fact, you are basically a very private individual who finds life's greatest rewards in solitude. You are emotionally attuned to a deep pulse of life, and so are not distracted by all the clamor and bustle of everyday existence in the world. You are always able to take time out within yourself – to tune in to how *you* really feel. This is not a self-pampering but on the contrary is an assertion of your own sense of personal fitness and belonging to the universe. Since you have no need to make apologies or excuses for yourself, your behavior is relatively free of the sorts of activities for which apologies and excuses are needed. You are clean and aboveboard in your relations with other people because you basically just want to feel good (about yourself and with them). This is not to imply that you are a patsy or pushover; you can be blunt and curt in resisting encroachment when the occasion requires it. You are a steadying and reassuring influence on other people because you are able to keep yourself on an even emotional keel no matter what is happening outside of you.

Mercury Unaspected – Candid

You are zestful about life and relationships, and at the same time are unpretentious and unassuming. Albeit animated and sociable, you are generally more interested in interacting with people – in examining and understanding their points of view and exchanging ideas with them – than you are in impressing them with your virtuosity. You learn a little something new about human nature from everybody you meet. You are frank (even shocking at times in your outspokenness), but this is the product of a spirit of camaraderie rather than designed to get a rise out of people. Because you are so upfront and nonjudgmental about yourself, you can afford to be nonjudgmental with others. Although you do have your preferences and prejudices in the abstract, you never hold them against the flesh-and-blood people you deal with in the here and now. The fact that you may be embroiled in a conflict with someone doesn't prevent you from seeing the situation from his or her side of the fence, or even from sympathizing with them (up to a point). You have a brightness, an unflagging optimism and sobriety, an ability to stop and *look* at things and other people, to appreciate what's going on, rather than to brush past life in a blind, oblivious rush.

Venus Unaspected – Genial

You are cheerful, prepossessing, and primarily attuned to that which is pure, lovely, and of good report. You possess a childlike artlessness and naturalness, not because you are naïve about what life is 'really like', but because you have an uncompromising determination to enjoy yourself and to keep your spirits high come what may. You know in your heart that life's rewards and pleasures are right there for the taking; you don't put a morass of complications (like feelings of guilt, shame, or lack of worth) in the path of your desires, but rather reach out unabashedly to take whatever you want from life without any need for coyness or pretense. You are open to receive from others (rather than impelled by a need to grab from them, as aspected Venus is) because you are moved by a genuine playfulness. You don't bog yourself down in tricky power manipulations since your only interest in other people is to feel good. If something isn't fun, or can't be made to be fun, then you don't much bother with it.

Mars Unaspected – Pert

You are daring, brash, cocky, and possess a hearty, devil-may-care personal manner. You are your own best friend – you have a genuine liking and enthusiasm for yourself – and the camaraderie between the two of you infects and excites other people as well. They find you charming and compelling precisely because you make no effort to attract notice or win them over, but rather you just fly with your impulses irregardless of where you might land. You are able to exercise bold decision because – although you may strut and swagger as much as any aspected Mars native – you are fundamentally self-starting and self-motivated rather than tangled up in the strings of social approval, security, worldly success and approbation, etc., which either hold people back by making them timid, or else trip them up by making them overbearing and overreaching. Although you are vigorous and dynamic, you are also steady and light of touch since there is really no emotional encouragement that you need from other people in order to proceed. You are a model of true abandonment – trust in the Spirit to catch you when you leap.

Jupiter Unaspected – Composed

You are relaxed and at your ease – just yourself – at all times. Although you are assertive and possess a strong sense of rightful place in the scheme of things, you are in no way aggressive, pushy, or inclined to elbow people out of your way. You have an innate sense that how you get there is more important than where you are going; you have no need to demonstrate that you are accomplishing anything in particular. You are not indolent – in fact, you burn inside with a driving enthusiasm and high energy – but you prefer to strike an easy, relaxed pace in life, to savor your experience like a fine wine. Even when you're zipping about you're never in a hurry, nor too busy to stop for other people and take their needs into account. You have a buoyant peppiness that inspires others with its can-do spunk. You also possess a nobility of spirit, an indomitable rectitude, which awes people and commands their respect. As you trust in the Spirit for your sustenance, you are able to sustain other people with your positive attitude and forbearance.

Saturn Unaspected – Tenacious
You are staunch, dogged, and are usually to be found off on some tangent of your own. You march to the music of a distant drum, and you possess a cheerful abstractedness and unvarnished forthrightness in your approach to other people. As stubborn and inflexible as they come, your combat is not with the world around you but with the weak and despised parts of your own personality. The central motif of your life is a burning drive to push your limits and to exceed your own expectations of yourself. This is not a competition with others (measuring yourself against them) but rather is a recognition of inner work to be done and a willingness to get on with it. Of all the unaspected planets, Saturn is the loneliest since you deny yourself all reliance upon other people – refuse all support – in order to find a sense of emotional reliance within yourself. You possess a true spirit of self-limitation and self-denial: although in most cases you are far from being a saint, nonetheless the potential is there. You are an example for others of resoluteness, persistence, and faith in the power of your own instincts.

Uranus Unaspected – Uninhibited
You are free-thinking and rebellious – not in the sense of rebelling *against*, but in the sense of feeling free to experiment and to fly with new ideas. You are blithely indifferent to what other people think about you – not as a pose (a cushion for their rejection) but rather as a springboard to taking risks and to truly enjoy yourself. You are probably no more

eccentric than anyone else, but you are unabashed about letting it all hang out. You have an air of conspiratorial mischief, of a kid up to no good, which appeals to other people and inclines them to indulge you in your quirks (as you indulge them in theirs). The crotchety, curt, impatient side of Uranus is softened by a distaste for bogging yourself down in other people's turmoil. Albeit volatile and no shrinking violet, you don't permit yourself to hold a grudge or to let other people pin you down or hold you back. You have a true grit, a mettle which carries the day with its sheer audacity and cool determination.

Neptune Unaspected – Deliberate
Since Neptune has been in sextile aspect to Pluto since the early 1940s, these planets have not been unaspected for over half a century. You are poised, confident, and dignified, and you possess an other-worldliness which operates 100% in the here and now. That is to say, you take pride in your adroitness, proficiency, and personal authority, but you act with the intuition that everyday life is just a dream, and therefore you can be emotionally removed from it. While you are anything but woolly or flaky – indeed, you are an acute observer of the everyday scene and miss none of life's nuances or fine details, and you act with an unerring sense of inner assurance – you nonetheless stand apart with a mood of preoccupation, indwelling, and rumination. This abstractedness is not a refusal to take responsibility for the world (as it is with an aspected Neptune), but rather is a true spirit of calm consideration, disinterestedness, professionalism, or art for art's sake. People naturally gravitate towards you because of your competence and command, which result from your ability to tune out static and listen to your own inner voice.

Pluto Unaspected – Observant
You have a dominating intensity, and you come on strong and sure of yourself; yet you also have a light touch and a good sense of humor. The cool, detached, Machiavellian analysis and calculation of Pluto is employed not for self-aggrandizement or power over others (as it is when Pluto is aspected), but rather is used for pure enjoyment. You have an oblique slant on the world, and you possess a gift for wry, sardonic, sassy banter. Precisely because you are so mentally clear and capable of spotting everyone's ego games and power moves, you tend to regard dog-eat-dog society as being too much of a hassle to get involved with, and

you decline to participate in it in any capacity except for that of the droll commentator on the sidelines. You are not lazy – indeed, you fairly buzz with energy – but you have so little worldly ambition that you put your intellect to work mocking society's norms of sedateness, reserve, and seriousness with your own nonchalance, rather than use it to advance in the world. You are a good example to others of how to keep things in perspective, how to avoid feeling offended by life and other people, and how to truly enjoy the ironies of existence.

4

Comparison of Different Canons of "Strength": Celestial State vs. Terrestrial State; Celestial State vs. Aspectual state; and Terrestrial State vs. Aspectual state

"If a benefic is in an unfavorable celestial and terrestrial state, its benefic rays do very little good, while its malefic rays do much harm." [Morinus Book 21, page 80]. "If both the celestial and terrestrial states of malefic planets are unfavorable, even their benefic rays are very harmful." [Morinus Book 21, page 81]. "Thus, Jupiter's trine from its domicile is the best, while its square from there is harmless or only very slightly harmful, while the trine from its exile is useless or only slightly helpful, while the square is harmful. And similarly, Saturn's trine from its domicile is beneficial while its square is not, while from its exile its trine is useless, even evil, and its square is quite pernicious. Of course, these general statements are valid only when other factors are equal." [Morinus Book 21, page 88].

What does it mean for the affairs of a given house when there are several planets in that house – particularly when some of them are stronger or weaker than others by sign, proximity to an angle, or by aspect? Morinus' answer to this question (and I agree) is that the different planets take on different meanings of that house: "When several planets are placed in the same house each of them acts in accordance with its nature and determinations both separately and in association with the other planets." [Morinus Book 21, page 52]. For example, I have Sun, Venus, and Mercury in the 9th house, and from my life circumstances (and a lifetime of observing transits, progressions and directions to and by these planets), I would say that the Sun in my 9th house refers to my interest in spiritual matters; Venus there means living in a foreign country and culture and having foreign partners; Mercury refers to my being a mathematician, programmer, astrologer, and writer. The Sun is in its ruling sign and angular, but very afflicted, thus I've had good luck in spiritual things (have made some incredible spiritual connections), but it's been a really hard row to hoe – unremitting struggle – and only sheer hubris and chutzpah have gotten me through the night (or, perhaps, brought it down upon myself). On the other hand, Mercury is well-aspected but cadent, so I've always excelled at academic and intellectual pursuits; nonetheless I am exaggeratedly self-conscious, neurotic, and paranoiac. Venus is peregrine, cadent, and afflicted – so, personal relationships (particularly with women) have been, for the most part, pretty disappointing, and I'm not exactly a fun person (having Sun conjunct Saturn and Pluto doesn't help).

The point is that each planet acts independently; several planets in the same house divide up the traditional significations of that house, and 'contradictory' indications don't contradict – they merely operate at different times, or with respect to different areas of life. Similarly, planets that are strong by one canon of strength and weak by another are effective in some respects but ineffectual in others, as we shall see in the interpretations which follow.

Celestial State vs. Terrestrial State

Terrestrial State has to do with getting one's way versus ceding the initiative: winning versus losing, whereas Celestial State has to do with self-satisfaction versus dissatisfaction: zestfulness versus resignation. Good Celestial State + Cadent implies that the natives shine on their own but don't readily fit into a group; Angular + Bad Celestial State implies that the natives are successful but lack much in the way of verve or enjoyment in what they are doing.

Sun Good Celestial State + Cadent = Resolute but Defensive Purpose
You are proud, unabashed, even a bit brazen and you possess a charming originality, sense of personal style. People admire your panache and your free-spirited impudence with life, even though they are sometimes put off by your strident assertiveness and overweening stubbornness, which can override people's sensibilities. Albeit somewhat lost without an audience to impress, you possess an idiosyncratic idealism and you always stick to your guns.

Sun Angular + Bad Celestial State = Self-Possessed but Temporizing Purpose

Although you are quite sociable, outgoing, and unabashed, you can easily fit yourself in to any social group; however in a close relationship you tend to be remote, vague, and evasive. You shy from intimacy and commitment, and in general you tend to lack a consistent sense of direction or application – perhaps you harbor unrealistic ambitions – or else you just live from one day to the next. You succeed in life on the strength of your finesse and skill at improvisation, at making the best of whatever opportunities are at hand.

Moon Good Celestial State + Cadent = Secure but Solipsistic Assurance

You are single-minded and conscientious, always attuned to your own instincts and intuition. You are basically a loner, following your own star rather than relying upon conventional wisdom or the views of other people. You have high hopes of yourself and other people, therefore you therefore easily feel betrayed, frustrated, or let down by events – constantly having to make downward revisions of your plans and hopes. But your earthy realism and sincerity win the respect of others.

Moon Angular + Bad Celestial State = Poised but Susceptible Assurance

You are artless and natural, always at your ease, and you do your own thing without shame or apology. You have a rather plaintive, long-suffering air, but your taciturn gruffness prevents others from showing you much in the way of sympathy. Albeit plainspoken and incapable of guile, you can also be quite highhanded and raw in dealing with people – arbitrary, quixotic, and fickle. On your positive side you have a feisty scrappiness which does lend you a certain charm.

Mercury Good Celestial State + Cadent = Clever But Awkward Mentality

You have a zesty *joie de vivre* which delights people with its naive optimism, idealism, and simplicity. Although you have a clear insight into other people's motives and a detached good-will, nonetheless your curt and zealous singlemindedness can give other people short shrift at times, leaving them feeling shunted aside or stepped on. You have the courage of your convictions, and you always charge full steam ahead.

Mercury Angular + Bad Celestial State = Convincing but Adamant Mentality

You are concentrated and painstaking, with a concentrated seriousness of mind which leads other people to accede to your wishes rather than to cross you or waste time in argument. You tend to be suspicious of other people's motives, and you rely upon no one's thinking but your own. Although you conceive of yourself as a down-to-earth realist, in fact you are not so much practical as positive and stubborn in your self-certainty, bowling people over rather than convincing them with logic.

Venus Good Celestial State + Cadent = Ingratiating but Calculating Enjoyment

You have a frank, unabashed, straightforward manner which charms and disarms people and inclines them to accede to your wishes. You know how to wheedle and finesse to get your way, but can be unreasoning and obdurate when you don't. You always know exactly how far you can go and what you can get away with.

Venus Angular + Bad Celestial State = Spontaneous but Finicky Enjoyment

You are plucky, game and ready to tackle anything. You relish challenge and have a bald, brash, even brazen certainty and finality. You must always be the leader or originator, and do things in your own way and your own time. Although you prefer to sidestep confrontation, you will always go right on ahead and do your own thing, rather than try to convince or to compromise.

Mars Good Celestial State + Cadent = Whole-Hearted but Malcontent Accomplishment

You have a sassy, ironic sense of humor and a sardonic view of life and your fellow bipeds. Although you are free-spirited and basically do your own thing come what may, you nonetheless have a tendency to grouse and complain. You are scrupulous in discharging – even exceeding – your obligations, but you also maintain a jealous watchfulness over whether others are pulling their share of the load as well. Although your everyday attitude is brisk and ready for anything, you often feel as though you are just drifting through life, or struggling on an endless treadmill – unrewarded and unfulfilled.

Mars Angular + Bad Celestial State = Plucky but Indecisive Accomplishment

You are outgoing and gregarious, with a sincere and unvarnished bonhomie – a gentility and nobility – which others find real and inviting. You tend to prefer consensus to initiative, and there may be an air of futility or resignation about you. You lack an underlying sense of conviction or self-certainty, so you can become overly dependent upon the cooperation of other people in order to get anything accomplished. You try to ameliorate rather than to challenge, and you are overly trusting and naive in your relationships. You have high expectations of yourself and equally high expectations of other people; but as a result you easily feel easily deceived or betrayed. When forced to take a stand you rely upon mulish obduracy rather than finesse to get your own way.

Jupiter Good Celestial State + Cadent = Disinterested but Cautious Understanding

You are fair and democratic, with considerable intellectual curiosity and an open-minded interest in others. You are a lively conversationalist and a boon companion – playful, good-humored, and willing to take things as they come. You live and let live, and always try to strike a harmonious balance, which on the negative side can make you overly reserved, noncommittal, and difficult to reach. You don't like getting too involved, and are inclined to turn aside from unpleasantness and complexity and seek a comfortable routine. You generally gravitate towards situations which offer little challenge, and so you tend to waste your talents and abilities, but you're usually quite content with yourself no matter what you are doing.

Jupiter Angular + Bad Celestial State = Enthusiastic but Preoccupied Understanding

You are cheerful, forward-looking, and optimistic, and can be quite sociable and glib. Although you try to play the hail-fellow-well-met, you nonetheless possess a nervous, skittish insecurity which employs whimsy and persiflage to maintain social control. You prefer not to reveal what you are actually thinking or feeling, but rather keep conversations and interactions on a superficial plane, so it can be hard to get a straight answer out of you. Yet you always look on the bright side and try to maintain a positive, hopeful attitude.

Saturn Good Celestial State + Cadent = Conscientious but Vague Responsibility
You are cool, competent, and sturdy, with an aloof or idiosyncratic air. Although you are sociable and possess a pleasant, agreeable personal manner, you nonetheless hark to a distant drum, so you are usually out of step or out of synch with what's going on around you. You may be a bit abstracted, unresponsive, or off on some cloud of your own. But you are highly idealistic, and upright and honorable in all your actions.

Saturn Bad Celestial State + Angular = Prissy but Firm Responsibility
You are single-minded and unyielding, a hard-charger who will not compromise or be deflected. You have an independent spirit and an unapologetic assertiveness of manner. Your wry, sharp, irreverent view of life and other people – and your positive self-certainty – can verge on tactlessness. There may be an overweening superiority or patronizing tendency, but your lack of subtlety and guile means that you can always be taken at your word.

Celestial State vs. Aspectual state

"When a planet is simultaneously both dignified and afflicted, it confers both good and evil, or difficulties and mixtures of fortune, according to the tenor of the aspects, by dint of their being fortunate or unfortunate." [Morinus Book 18, page 64]. "If both planets are posited in their respective Detriment or Fall, they will be quite potent in producing a pernicious effect, especially by a bad aspect, and will be incapable of producing any good, even by a good aspect. If only one of the planets is located in its Detriment or Fall, that (debilitated) planet would impede the effect of the other." [Morinus Book 18, page 67]. "Both planets being peregrine will signify a weakness of performance and an impoverishment of the means to accomplish the ends." [Morinus Book 18, page 67].

Any planet in Good Celestial State + Afflicted radiates confidence and sureness of purpose and plan, but at the same time it possesses a tendency to withdraw – to go its own way – rather than to cooperate or collaborate with others. On the other hand, any planet Well-aspected + Bad Celestial State is flexible and can easily adapt itself to the necessities of other people and the social environment in which it finds itself, but it tends to be timid or hesitant in its outreach.

Sun Good Celestial State + Afflicted = Spirited but Resistant Purpose
You are strong-willed, self-assured, and independent of spirit, but are too uncompromising and unyielding for collaborative effort. You tend to go off on your own tangent rather than get bogged down in discussions or compromises, which rarely redound to your benefit in any case. You are a proud loner, with a smug and haughty independence, and you disdain the support of others rather than modify your own (somewhat quixotic) ideals one iota.

Sun Well-aspected + Bad Celestial State = Aloof but Temporizing Purpose
You relate well in groups because you are open to new ideas and do not insist on taking the lead. You tend to stay in the background and watch and wait your opportunity, rather than to vaunt yourself and invite conflict. You are low-key and stealthy rather than demonstrative, and you accomplish your ends by quiet persistence and diligence rather than by wielding power overtly. Because you are always willing to understand other people's points of view and to take them into account, you are able to easily enlist the cooperation of others. However, you are often unclear in your own mind as to what your goals are – are indecisive or disorganized – and so prefer to hang back rather than put your ego on the line.

Moon Good Celestial State + Afflicted = Secure but Moody Assurance
You take things as they come and manage to keep on an even emotional keel by turning aside and seeking solace within yourself. You are basically solitary, even standoffish, and don't let other people or circumstances get to you or knock you off your pins. You can be overly remote, stodgy, and unmovable. You take pride in your independence of spirit and have learned not to depend or rely too much on others.

Moon Well-aspected + Bad Celestial State = Blithe but Susceptible Assurance
Although you possess a cheeky insouciance and a light and buoyant demeanor, you are actually quite vulnerable emotionally and you take things very much to heart. You try not to show what you are actually

feeling inside, and your cavalier manner and impudent dismissal of people's feelings can make them feel neglected or slighted. Nonetheless you maintain an eager expectancy and you don't permit anyone to bring you down.

Mercury Good Celestial State + Afflicted = Clever but Dogmatic Mentality

You are sharp and sharp-tongued and you are nobody's fool. You are quick to pick up on nuances and subtleties and quick to react to them. You don't shy from disputation since you hold your own viewpoint to be paramount and irrefutable: you are certain in your beliefs and opinions, and are forthright in expressing them. You hold to your own course rather than adapt to circumstances. You're always willing to put your ideas on the line and to rely on your own perspicacity rather than to compromise with anyone or to accept anything short of your own ideal.

Mercury Well-aspected + Bad Celestial State = Nimble but Adamant Mentality

You are sociable and gregarious, and you possess a sprightly, mischievous good humor which disarms people and inclines them to indulge you. You find it very necessary to win other people's favor and acceptance in order to vindicate you own viewpoint, since you are never altogether sure where you stand. You easily fall into mental ruts since it is difficult for you to take contradiction objectively, or to learn anything from criticism. You can evince a perverse and bullheaded streak – reflexively defending your own point of view against all comers. But you are admirably forthright and always try to appeal to other people's better side.

Venus Good Celestial State + Afflicted = Ingratiating but Broody Enjoyment

You are outgoing, make good eye contact, and get on a personal basis with people immediately. You are artless, candid, forthright, and lay all your cards on the table. However, you also lack objectivity, and you take any dissent as bad faith on the other person's part. People's reactions often puzzle you, since you believe you are acting with the best interests of everyone in mind. You can assume or presume too much – presupposing agreement rather than listening to other viewpoints – and thus generate conflict and rebuff in spite of your best of intentions. However your well-meaning guilelessness inclines people to give you the benefit of the doubt.

Venus Well-aspected + Bad Celestial State = Perky but Finicky Enjoyment

You have a rather brash and forward manner, and you are quite adept at finagling and finessing to get your own way. You are shrewd and sensitive to other people's limits and you have a realistic appraisal of what you can solicit or get away with. Although you prefer concord and thus always try to please and be pleasing, nonetheless you are quite capable of bowling people over when you can't win them over or go around them somehow. Your reliance on bluff impudence and hubris, and your fidelity to your own designs, give you an air of authority not to be trifled with.

Mars Good Celestial State + Afflicted = Whole-Hearted but Ornery Accomplishment

You possess a good-humored audacity and spirit of derring-do which can be very charming in their proper moment. However, your cocksure self-assurance and brash swagger can wear thin on people constantly exposed to your bumptiousness, or those who have to work *with* you rather than *under* you (you are magnanimous with people you consider your inferiors). You love to argue, and you have a genius for niggling wrongheadedness – scoring points for yourself rather than working things out. Although inclined to pose and strut, you nonetheless are courageous and outfront, and you are in your element when bold action is called for.

Mars Well-aspected + Bad Celestial State = Efficient but Indecisive Accomplishment

You possess a self-conscious, inoffensive, and unassuming personality. You don't make waves or attract undue attention to yourself, but rather try to ingratiate yourself with and to please other people. You are diplomatic and politic, and you shun or ameliorate conflict wherever possible. On the other hand, you can be overly neutral or vacillating when definiteness and commitment are called for. But you are straightforward, aboveboard, and always on the square.

Jupiter Good Celestial State + Afflicted = Disinterested but Contrary Understanding

You have a staunchly independent detachment and you always march to the beat of a distant drum. Your idiosyncratic arbitrariness and headstrong whimsicality are carried off in good humor, but you often strike others as being self-satisfied and unreachable. You tune in completely to your own wavelength, and evince a cheerful obliviousness to everything else. On your positive side, you mean what you say, and you unabashedly do your own thing and go your own way with verve, style, and panache.

Jupiter Well-aspected + Bad Celestial State = Ingenuous but Preoccupied Understanding

You are circumspect and wary of people, and therefore you always strain to make a good impression and to adapt yourself to the person you are with. You are frank, plainspoken, and unabashedly sincere; you want other people to believe you, and they do, because of your openness and down-to-earth practicality. Nonetheless, there is a perfunctoriness or abstraction about you which doesn't achieve a great deal of depth or sense of real contact in your daily relationships. But you are a sympathetic listener, always solicitous for the well-being of others, and you possess a simple and open manner which inspires trust.

Saturn Good Celestial State + Afflicted = Conscientious but Bull-Headed Responsibility

You are fiercely independent and uncompromising of spirit, and are fearless in blazing new trails through life rather than treading the straight and narrow. You tend to distrust 'the system', and you refuse to play by anyone's rules but your own. You are a loner, distrustful of sharing your feelings or becoming dependent on others. You are scrupulous and competent, but you have a supercilious and contemptuous dismissal of people who don't measure up to your own high standards. You are brusque, bullheaded, and rely upon pigheaded obstinacy to force other people to give up or give way in despair.

Saturn Well-aspected + Bad Celestial State = Ready but Prissy Responsibility

You are companionable and loquacious, with an ironic sense of humor and an irreverent view of the passing scene. You have a cool, calm, magisterial presence – the sense that you are on top of things and in command – which compels the recognition and respect of other people. However, you can also be quite haughty, and your chintzy sang-froid can be annoyingly trifling or frivolous – not taking other people seriously. You maintain your equanimity by not getting too involved or committed.

Terrestrial State vs. Aspectual state

Both angular and well-aspected planets show lucky attitudes, but angularity is more of an aristocratic, born-to-rule, noblesse oblige – a sense of fitness. By contrast, well-aspected planets show how easily natives make things click for themselves in everyday situations and relationships by adapting themselves; by adjusting or avoiding as need be, rather than by brazening their way through (as angular planets tend to do).

Quite a bit of detail can be extracted from this sort of analysis. For example Sun Angular + Afflicted can mean conflict with the father or husband (depending upon which angle is involved); Moon Angular + Afflicted can mean conflict with the mother or wife, etc.

Sun Angular + Afflicted = Self-Possessed but Resistant Purpose

You are proud – a bit haughty even – and you cut an independent swath through life. You tend to be finicky, and are quite impatient with other people. Your rather impudent and autocratic stance naturally tends to ruffle other people's feathers, but you need very little in the way of support or succor, and don't care much what other people think. At your best your fierce individualism is a model which others look up to.

Sun Well-aspected + Cadent = Defensive but Aloof Purpose

You are a watcher and listener, who observes the scene very carefully before taking action or committing yourself. Although you are sociable and ingratiating, nonetheless you often feel like an outsider vis a vis other people – at a loss; not quite in tune with where they are coming from. As a result you tend to measure yourself against their responses, and either cut and trim to try to fit in, or else turn your back and walk away. You try to hold yourself above reproach by doing more than is really necessary.

Moon Angular + Afflicted = Poised but Moody Assurance

You are emotionally independent and self-sustaining, with a remote, pensive, above-it-all air. You have a self-obsessed, hermit-like tendency – or at least an appreciation for solitude – and you keep your balance by withdrawing from unpleasantness. Intimacy is difficult because you tend to be thin-skinned and touchy – quick to react and quick to take umbrage – and you don't readily share your feelings. You find it easiest to just do things on your own.

Moon Well Aspected + Cadent = Blithe but Solipsistic Assurance
You are gregarious and solicitous, but also capricious and whimsical; you are usually off following your own star, or buzzing around with a bee in your bonnet. You are just not *there* a lot of the time. You brim with ideas and plans and projects, but don't have a consistent follow-through or a realistic view of the potentials, thus you often find your hopes dashed in spite of your best intentions. But you can quickly pick yourself up again and dash off in some new direction.

Mercury Angular + Afflicted = Convincing but Dogmatic Mentality
You are independent-minded, self-assured, and possess considerable bravado. You always know you're right: you neither require nor listen to input from anyone else in formulating your plans and projects. You are cool and impassive, and are relatively indifferent to what anyone thinks or feels about you. Because you feel little need to prove anything to anyone and have little interest in communicating, other people find you hard to reach and thorny to deal with; but you always remain true to yourself.

Mercury Well-aspected + Cadent = Nimble but Awkward Mentality
You are shrewd and clever, you try to be lively and witty in order to win other people over. Although you are mentally clear and quick to pick up on nuances, you are very self-conscious and sensitive to how other people see you – and so very easily taken aback and offended. You mull and sulk over every little contretemps, and can be quite blunt, brusque, and sharp-tongued in your own defense. Albeit huffy and easily bent out of shape, you have a wry sense of humor and an ironic view of life.

Venus Angular + Afflicted = Spontaneous but Broody Enjoyment
You possess a supreme self-possession and a regal bearing no matter what company you find yourself in. But together with your noblesse oblige, you have an air of complacent superiority and blasé indifference. You have a saucy mischievousness when you are bent on your own designs, but you can also be quite touchy and grumpy, pulling away from people when

they make demands on you. Your blithe nonchalance and snootiness can become infuriating – as if you are saying that it's never your problem. But your élan and unwillingness to let other people bog you down keep you on an even emotional keel even when everyone else is freaking out.

Venus Well-aspected + Cadent = Perky but Calculating Enjoyment
You are light of spirit and maintain a pleasant, approachable front even when you are inwardly simmering and gritting your teeth. You are outgoing, sociable, and don't like to make waves, nonetheless you tend to be suspicious of other people's motives and inclined to disbelieve their self-presentation (perhaps because you don't quite believe your own). You can be quite critical and fault-finding, but you manifest it by implication and nuance rather than risk open confrontation; you skitter away from any sort of conflict if you can possibly avoid it. You try to keep things flowing easily and evenly at all times.

Mars Angular + Afflicted = Plucky but Ornery Accomplishment
You are bluff, short, impatient, and trenchant – utterly lacking in subtlety, social grace or niceties. You are glib and frank, with nothing to hide or apologize for, and at times you can be gratuitously brusque and abrasive. You possess a cocksure insolence which ploughs its own furrow in life and has no thoughts or worries about consequences. You are highly individualistic with an original point of view – off on your own vision quest and determined to keep free of any constraint or restriction.

Mars Well-aspected + Cadent = Efficient but Malcontent Accomplishment
You are easily annoyed and tend to keep up a running commentary of complaints about other people's failings and the ills of the world, but you nonetheless always maintain your cool and don't allow people's antics or adverse circumstances get you into a sweat. You keep yourself under tight control, and your forbidding reserve and critical mindset tend to keep other people from tangling with you. You are imperturbable, impassive, and go about your business with a minimum of pother.

Jupiter Angular + Afflicted = Enthusiastic but Contrary Understanding
You possess a bold dynamism and, devil-may-care cheekiness; you immediately roll up your sleeves and take charge in any situation. Your breezy optimism and considerable personal charm and panache just bowl

people right over. There's something of the used-car salesman about your self-presentation: insistent, overconfident, overweening. You must always be the leader, never the follower, but for the most part people are ready to cede you pride of place and let you do your thing unimpeded (rather than try to contradict you or head you off).

Jupiter Well-aspected + Cadent = Ingenuous but Cautious Understanding

You are straightforward and unvarnished in manner and you make good eye-contact, so people are inclined to trust you and your motives and lean towards helping you out. You take a sympathetic interest in the well-being of others, and you go out of your way to help them whenever possible. However you can also be quite self-absorbed and focused on your own ends and point of view; beneath your friendliness you are unshakeable in your convictions – immovable and intransigent. There is something of the politician about your self-presentation in the way you convince yourself by convincing other people. Your high-mindedness and genuine idealism win others to your side.

Saturn Angular + Afflicted = Firm but Bull-Headed Responsibility

You have an adamant, dig-in-your-heels stubbornness and fixity of purpose which none can deflect. You are completely focused upon the path beneath your feet, and once your mind is made up there's really no point in talking to you. You are punctilious in carrying out your responsibilities but you yourself must decide yourself where these will lie. You do not conform to what is expected by others, and you must always stand up for yourself (since no one else will). On your positive side you need little in the way of support from anyone, and you never say die.

Saturn Well-aspected + Cadent = Ready but Vague Responsibility

You have a simple, straightforward sincerity and eagerness, together with a somewhat woolly innocence or naiveté about people. You are candid and transparent, and try to appeal to people's good faith and common sense. As a result you can be overly trusting, or too ready to yield ground or bend yourself out of shape to please others. You depend upon a network of allies and supporters in order to keep your own balance and measure how well you are doing. You are unnerved by conflict and you try to maintain your humor and equanimity through a studied aloofness or indefiniteness, keeping your eyes over the horizon and your head in the clouds.

Uranus Angular + Afflicted = Outspoken but Rebellious Independence

You are single-minded, fearless, and vociferous and possess a wild, unconventional streak. You are quick to make a stand, and are always ready to go to bat for the weak and helpless. Although you don't go out of your way to seek conflict, you certainly don't shrink from it either. You chafe at direction and restriction, and at your worst you can be very capricious and dictatorial, or else try to get your way by fiat or fait accompli. Your high-minded (if self-serving) idealism lends a nobility to your character and your doughty bravado is a model of fierce individualism.

Uranus Well-aspected + Cadent = Hearty but Cagey Independence

You are good-natured, complaisant, and optimistic about your prospects. Although you have a highly original point of view and slant on things, nonetheless you try to work with others and within established frameworks insofar as is possible. You try to be reasonable and conciliatory in your dealings with others, taking their interests and viewpoints into account when formulating plans of your own. You incline to take things in your stride; you don't let yourself get into a sweat or an uproar, and you uphold standards of fair play in your own conduct. You are more interested in the art of the possible – in getting things done in an orderly fashion with a minimum of pother – than you are in making a personal statement.

Neptune Angular + Afflicted = Certain but Wary Intuition

You are extremely serious, determined, and focused. You trust no one, but respond only to your own inner urgings. You are impatient with people and don't even make a pretense of listening to anyone or heeding advice. You are close-mouthed, gruff, and indomitable, with a fierce – even fearsome – aspect, so people are afraid to cross you or get in your way. At the same time you are highly visionary, and are not motivated by the things which motivate most people. You maintain your staunch idealism and hopefulness in the face of any challenge.

Neptune Well-aspected + Cadent = Trusting but Worried Intuition

You are guided by faith in abstract standards of fair play and are scrupulous in following the rules and fulfilling expectations. You are high-principled and also a bit self-righteous; you are zealous in observing whether other people are upholding their share of the bargain, and you look down your nose at those whom you feel are shirking. You feel under a special incumbency to justify your own worth by serving or yielding ground to others. Because you are extremely sensitive to rebuff, you tend to be defensive and conciliatory even beyond the point of comfort, then you blow up or complain that you are being taken advantage of. But your insistence on honorably acquitting yourself is a model of patient forbearance.

Pluto Angular + Afflicted = Uncompromising but Obsessive Clarity
You have a sharp, shrewd, critical mind which sees beneath superficial appearances and which is quick to spot errors and failings in other people's thinking. You have a capricious, idiosyncratic, nonconformist spirit, which on its negative side tends towards a willful obstinacy or barefaced effrontery. You are audacious and defiant, and you insist on getting your own way by bulling your way through with contemptuous superiority. Your sardonic and devil-may-care insolence and megalomania floor people and incline them to step out of your way.

Pluto Well-aspected + Cadent = Apropos but Doubtful Clarity
You are retiring and observant rather than pushy or assertive. You have a softness which invites collaboration rather than trying to dominate other people – perhaps overstepping yourself or making an error. You are restrained and diplomatic, always watching, listening, and evaluating rather than charging ahead on your own. On the other hand you can be noncommittal, vacillating, and a bit of a pushover when confronting people who are surer of themselves and what they are after than you are. But you always strive for consensus and take into account what is best for all concerned.

5

Other Dignities

Retrogradation and Station

> In Chapter IX of Book 18 Morinus states with regard to the planets:
> "When swift in motion, they indicate the quickness of the habits,
> actions, or effects of any of the significators; when slow in motion,
> their sluggishness; when of average motion, an intermediate state.
> Furthermore, when direct, they foretell the continuance and
> progression of the effects; when retrograde, their interruption or lack
> of completion; when stationary, their slowness but also their stability
> and durability." [Morinus Book 18, page 50].

The phenomenon of retrogradation occurs when the earth 'overtakes'
a planet in its orbit, so from the point of view of an observer on earth
the planet appears to stop and then move backwards in the zodiac. The
astrological meaning of a retrograde planet is that the impulse symbolized
by that planet is attuned not to the world of people, but to the world of
inner feeling. The influence is not so much unsocial as unsocialized,
operating in the realm of intuition rather than that of social obligations
and restraints.

In spite of all the indoctrination children receive in the effort to
civilize them, almost everyone escapes into adulthood with at least
some of their spontaneity intact, and there is nothing quite so endearing
and frustrating about other people as their erratic impulses, their
unpredictability. In the horoscope, this impulsiveness is symbolized by
the retrograde planets.

The retrograde planet responds instinctively, with supreme faith and
supreme gall. It represents a highly original and idiosyncratic streak in the
native. There is an unsophisticated cockiness here which is not without
its charm, but which is the positive side of a naïve solipsism that can

also create difficulties in communicating with other people whenever the impulse symbolized by the retrograde planet is brought into play. The childlike impulsiveness is coupled with a lack of sensitivity to the minimum requirements of social constraint. There is often a brusque, outspoken, roughshod tendency which can leave other people feeling bruised. In this area of life, at least, the natives are so sure of themselves that they will listen to no one, nor will they learn from past experience or even stop and think. Intuitive impulse is far more persuasive than logic. Sometimes the natives are brilliantly correct, and at other times they're merely pigheaded; but they rarely show the capacity for distinguishing between the two. Their motto is, "Damn the torpedoes, full speed ahead."

I would not call retrogradation a strength factor per se; it depends upon your point of view. Consider Mercury retrograde: this indicates a mentality which is impulsive and capricious, which acts on whim with utter self-certainty and conviction, with little regard for the consequences. But at the same time there is very little self-reflection, objectivity, or ability to understand other people's viewpoints – these natives have very little finesse or diplomacy. Mercury retrograde natives are deaf to other people's opinions and points of view and insensitive to their feelings. They are unable to work cooperatively since they tend to elbow other people aside. Thus Mercury retrograde can be considered a decided debility with regard to personal relationships and collaborative effort.

On the other hand, Mercury retrograde is decisive, gritty, single-minded, and willing to take risks and fly with its impulses. Mercury retrograde natives have a gift for focusing their attention entirely on the matter or project of the moment, to the exclusion of any other consideration or competing demand, which gives them a genius for handily accomplishing things which other people would deem impossible. So, with regard to worldly accomplishment and realization of desires and ambitions, then Mercury retrograde must be considered quite strong. And so on, with the other retrograde planets. So, we can conclude that retrogradation strengthens some aspects of planetary functioning and weakens others.

Note that in Vedic astrology retrogradation is considered a definite strength factor, known as *Chesta Bala*. Stated simply, the idea is that the 'more retrograde' a planet is, the higher its *Chesta Bala* strength.[1] This is a good example of how Vedic and occidental astrology take decidedly different views of what the term 'strength' means (another is the fact mentioned previously that both systems use the same tables of celestial strength, but the longitudes involved are presently shifted by a full sign).

Robert De Luce says of *Chesta Bala* that "Chesta may be likened to a person either racing through life's experiences without gaining much spiritual or intellectual insight, or to one who moves slowly and methodically, gaining much in knowledge of how to handle karmic situations."[2] However, I believe this is incorrect; as noted above, in my purview Mercury retrograde natives are the ones who learn the least from their experience since they are incapable of objective insight or listening to other people. They just keep making the same mistakes over and over and any difficulties they encounter are always the other guy's fault. My own (and, apparently, Morinus') view of the strength/debility conferred by retrogradation is thus diametrically opposite to that of De Luce: that it is the retrograde planets which are so fixated upon their own purposes and the path beneath their feet as to often miss out on what is going on around them (although in the cases of Uranus, Neptune, and Pluto this is strengthening).

We can consider that retrogradation is a mild debility for the planets from Mercury through Saturn, and a mild dignity for Uranus, Neptune, and Pluto. This is because all three of the trans-Saturnian planets have a somewhat 'retrograde' meaning to begin with: they are more attuned to unconscious rather than conscious motivation. Thus when one of these three planets is retrograde its operation is enhanced rather than distorted. However, station is a very powerful dignity for all the planets.

---

1. For details, see page 61ff of *Graha and Bhava Balas*, by B.V. Raman, Sri Rajeswari, Bangalore 1970, which propounds a calculation for *Chesta Bala* based upon the planet's position in mean longitude (its perihelion longitude + its mean anomaly). Like other Vedic strength calculations, *Chesta Bala* is carried out to three decimal place accuracy – a remarkable degree of precision which we poor occidental astrologers must surely envy.

2. De Luce, Robert, *Constellational Astrology*, De Luce Publishing, LA, 1963, page 34.

Preponderance of Retrogrades

When there is a preponderance of retrograde planets (5 or more) in your horoscope, you have an unaffected impulsiveness. You put out the minimum amount of conformity necessary for survival in your social milieu, but you don't really plug yourself into it. You are not animated by the customary expectations of reward for the sacrifice of your own individuality for the group good. You are a maverick, a renegade, armored in obstinacy and determined to carve out your own niche. As a result your life may tend to lack cohesion and direction; it has an improvised, patchy or makeshift quality which results from living by feel rather than by plan. You have a burning need for emotional privacy which manifests as emotional imperviousness. You are not so much rude as rough in your handling of people; too bent upon your own fancies to pay much mind to the sensibilities of others. A preponderance of retrogrades can be either an uninhibited psychological freedom or a lack of common sense and perspective.

Absence of Retrogrades

When no planets in your horoscope are retrograde, you tend to distrust your own intuitive impulses, hence your acts lack the assurance of inner certainty. You are not so much repressed as out of touch with your inner feelings. You avoid making impulsive errors by avoiding impulse: you are too easily swayed by logic, by your conscious mind, to put much stake in following your heart. You try to base your behavior on abstract standards of fairness and reasonableness. You go out of your way to reconcile conflict and maintain some semblance of accord, and you are nonplussed by emotional undercurrents. You are overly compliant because you never feel you're standing on solid ground; thus you are easily imposed upon or taken advantage of by others who are more sure of what it is they want.

Mercury Retrograde

With Mercury retrograde in your horoscope your mind – your self-consciousness, self-images, self-reflection – is highly attuned to subconscious impulse. To other people you often seem out of it, or off on some tangent of your own, blissfully oblivious in your own little bubble. In the course of the average day, any number of whims and fancies dart into the mind of the average person, but only rarely will he or she act on one, since to do so entails getting sidetracked from the larger issues of life. However, to you Mercury retrograde natives there are no larger issues; rather, the larger issue is the freedom to be able to act on whim. You seem to others to have no sense of discrimination between the important and the unimportant, you only care about the principle of the thing, about being right, and in your mind you are always right. You make issues out of things which no one else considers significant, and you steamroll over the logic and sensibilities of anyone in your way. Since you are oblivious to the second thoughts or fear of consequences which daunt most people, you have a knack for getting things to click your way. You have unshakeable trust in the certainty of your inmost feelings.

Venus Retrograde

With Venus retrograde your desire nature – your need for appreciation and reward – is self-fulfilling and narcissistic. You have extremely acute perceptions and refined sensibilities. You are poised and composed, with a strong sense of your rightful place in the scheme of things. You are consciously responsive to undercurrents and you have an incisive and cynical sense of humor – a skepticism which sees through all the power ploys and machinations of everyday society. You may consider yourself to be above the petty intrigues and jockeying for position, since your sense of self-worth comes from within and needs little reassurance from others. You don't marry, for example, for the usual reasons people marry – you may do it for convenience, or because it's expected of you, but never to compensate for an inner emotional lack or need for security. Nonetheless you have your own ulterior motives to which you can be quite blind; you are captivated by your own acumen and can withdraw into a vain and prissy self-pampering or a callous indifference. Your stiff propriety demands special consideration and privileges from others.

Mars Retrograde

With Mars retrograde in your horoscope you have a bold, dogged, and aggressive side which is capricious and wild. You are headstrong and intransigent in pursuing your own ends. You stand on your sense of personal honor, and you manifest a single-minded rigidity and persistence in your wishful thinking which can wear anyone down to acquiescence. You zealously defend your own prerogatives against encroachment, and become adamant and touchy whenever you feel you are being prodded.

You are not so much uncooperative as you are focused on your own goals, and you can be vague and elusive whenever outside demands are placed on you. You are strong-willed and have a well-developed sense of personal obligation, but also an overweening rebelliousness and wrong-headed contumacy. Although you often strike other people as being disorganized or overly fond of a comfortable rut, you have an unflinching determination with which you muddle through any difficulty.

Jupiter Retrograde

With Jupiter retrograde in your horoscope your joviality – your buoyant, gregarious, and expansive side – operates in purely unconditioned fashion. There is a complete lack of pretense or guile here, but also a lack of refinement and sensitivity. You are amiable (albeit bluff) in speech and manner and have an earthy good humor, but the reverse side of your delightful candor is an incapacity for comprehending subtleties or taking an unprejudiced point of view. You see everything in terms of black or white: you are intolerant of disagreement, are easily affronted, and are unable to compromise. You get huffy at the least slight and you are completely unaware of the effect which your own offhanded behavior and attitudes have on other people. Your smug superiority is inextricably entwined with your unalloyed optimism and enthusiasm.

Saturn Retrograde

With Saturn retrograde in your horoscope your serious, dignified and deliberate side operates in a highly intuitive fashion. In contrast with Saturn direct types who are less self-disciplined and respond primarily to limitations imposed by the outside world, you retrograde types have a strong inner sense of justice and fairness, and you pride yourself on your self-restraint and your adherence to principle. You insist on defining where your own responsibilities will lie. You are hard-working and don't do things the easy way or by half-measures. Albeit undeniably upright and honest, you possess a fierce sense of rectitude which can become a narrow-minded absolutism. Since you eschew outside restriction (together with its rewards) in favor of voluntary self-limitation, you warrant yourself to be incorruptible. You believe you stand for the moral right; that only your motives are indisputably pure and disinterested. It can be quite a thorny matter to deal with such a bastion of righteousness, no matter how sincere you may be.

Uranus Retrograde

With Uranus retrograde in your horoscope you are amicable and candid –
a strange combination of affability and orneriness. You are a sympathetic
listener and have a feeling for the common people and a philosophy
of live and let live. You grant others the liberty to be themselves, and
you demand the same right in return. However your democratic exterior
conceals an extreme self-will; an intentness and an intolerance of being
crossed. Although you are intense, even driven, you are both reserved
and stoical. You are a stickler for your private space and beneath the
friendliness there is a low growl which is not to be ignored. You can
be quite the prima donna – self-dramatizing, fastidious and persnickety.
You are idealistic and fraternal, but are also a paradigm of staunch
individualism.

Neptune Retrograde

With Neptune retrograde your intuitive and other-worldly side is
particularly prone to flight. You are optimistic, plain-spoken, and
straightforward, with an off-the-cuff manner and an unselfconscious
simplicity and ease. You have a naïve cocksureness about yourself;
you are pert and cheeky, with an idealistic slant on life. However the
other side of your naturalness and delicacy of feeling is a nonchalant
perfunctoriness. You are tuned in to your own private wavelength and
can be quite heedless of other people's feelings when you are in pursuit
of your own fancies. You are not so much insensitive as overly subjective
and inclined to view matters with your own rose-colored lenses. You
manifest a pigheaded wistfulness behind your façade of sprightly charm.

Pluto Retrograde

With Pluto retrograde in your horoscope you are brazen and willful,
with a facility for cutting across nonsense and getting down to business.
You are assertive and blunt, and communicate with people directly,
without the veneer of social polish or artificial manners. You have your
own flamboyant personal style of which you are quite proud – that of a
canny operator, someone who is in the know and is not to be trifled with.
However, the other side of your sassiness is an overbearing self-certainty,
a scornfulness which pulls away from people or else bowls them right
over with its aristocratic superiority. Your bravado is the unavoidable
byproduct of your can-do pluckiness.

Station

Where retrogradation is not an unequivocal strength factor per se, the state of being *stationary* – no matter whether Stationary Direct (oriental) or Stationary Retrograde (occidental) – must be reckoned a very important strength factor. When a planet is stationary (that is, when the birth occurred within three days of the exact date when the planet changed direction), the impulse symbolized by the planet has the same conscious responsiveness to deep-seated feelings as the planet when retrograde, and it can be equally stubborn and self-obsessed. But the stationary planet is more alert, astute, and aware – more willing to rely upon reason as well as intuition. The stationary planet moves deftly through life, avoiding as much entangling compromise as possible, whereas the retrograde planet just blunders ahead. *Stationary* is similar in meaning to *unaspected* in the sense that both increase the planet's independence of action (not caring what other people think or do). Both of these dignities release the native from societal imperatives (at least insofar as the action of that planet is concerned), and give greater intuitive (or quixotic) expression to the planet. Any individual stationary planet wields a great deal of control – is decisive, clear, and winning – with regard to the aspect of life symbolized by that planet (and its house position and aspects).

The two stations are quite different in character: Stationary Retrograde is strict, taciturn, stiff-necked – it digs in its heels and makes a stand. Stationary Direct is easy-going and laid-back – it avoids being pinned down by slithering around commitment. But both types are alike in their nimble sense of balance and their immovability.

Keywords for the Stations

SD = Blithe, Noncommittal   SR = Hard, Stubborn

Mercury Stationary

When Mercury is stationary in your horoscope you possess all the whimsy of the Mercury retrogrades, and you are equally impervious, but you are more aware of feelings and nuances than you let on. Together with bullheaded obstinacy your arsenal contains astuteness, cunning, and a sense of the politic – you know exactly what you can get away with. You may affect indifference and standoffishness, and you can be maddeningly imperturbable. While you are punctilious in discharging your chosen duties, you can be mulishly begrudging of your energies beyond this point, no matter what the situation may seem to be demanding. You basically just want to be left alone to do your own thing.

Venus Stationary

If Venus is stationary in your horoscope you are as emotionally self-sufficient as the Venus Retrograde types, and possess the same above-it-all *sang-froid*. Yet you are more personal and approachable than the stuffy Venus Retrograde types without being any more warm or intimate. You revel in your own sense of fitness, and have considerable personal flair and magnetism. You possess a smug nonchalance – the sort of detached aplomb which characterizes the born aristocrat. You have little interest in whether or not you are understood or appreciated by other people; those who do (the elect) do, and those who don't (the rabble) don't, and that's that. Your sense of self-worth comes from within – it doesn't depend upon your current status. You are as self-possessed and self-sufficient as the retrograde types but are far more down to earth and inviting.

Mars Stationary

With Mars stationary in your horoscope you are as rebellious as the retrograde type and have the same pioneering self-sufficiency, but you are lighter and more sociable in your instincts. You have a spirit of playfulness and mischief that is missing in the concentrated retrograde type. You know how to wheedle and cajole, but you also know how to browbeat when the need arises. Your capricious self-will is made more palatable by your daring and saucy impudence.

Jupiter Stationary

With Jupiter stationary in your horoscope you can be as opinionated and supercilious as Jupiter retrograde, but you are far shrewder. You are deft at parrying arguments with your wry humor, and you are the master of the sardonic retort – more the wiseacre than the good ole boy. Albeit far more articulate in your stonewalling than the retrograde type, you are no less dogmatic; you are fascinated by your own adroitness.

Saturn Stationary

With Saturn stationary in your horoscope you are no more tractable than the retrograde type, yet you have a great deal more finesse and diplomacy. You make allowances for other people, and are not as quick on the indignation trigger. You are not so much modest as unobtrusive and wary. Unswerving in your imperatives, you nonetheless thread your way around people by not presuming too much or overstepping yourself. The stiff dignity of retrograde Saturn is here tempered by a sense of the politic.

Uranus Stationary
With Uranus stationary in your horoscope you possess the same gumption as the retrograde type, but you are jauntier, more audacious and freewheeling. You are insolent with life, craving challenge and flaunting your indomitability. You can be as severe and heavy-handed as the retrograde type, but are far more blithe and insouciant.

Neptune Stationary
With Neptune stationary in your horoscope you possess the same fanciful abstractedness and sanguine self-assurance as the retrograde type, but with a sharper sense of pragmatism and expedience. Where the Neptune retrograde type brims with vague yearnings, you readily act yours out. You usually seek some sheltered nook in life wherein your competence is undisputed and your own vagaries hold sway. The breeziness of retrograde Neptune becomes a headstrong refractoriness at the station.

Pluto Stationary
With Pluto stationary in your horoscope you are more sedate than the retrograde type, but no less bullheaded. You are more focused and intent than blatant or ostentatious. Plain speaking and plain dealing, you are willing to give ground on nonessentials, and you are generally more interested in being heard than in demonstrating your virtuosity. Your spunkiness is tempered by a down-to-earth practicality.

Synodic Phase
Morinus devotes an entire chapter to the strength planets receive vis a vis their position in their orbits around the Sun (whether oriental or occidental). In Chapter VIII of Book 18 Morinus quotes Ptolemy that planets rising before the Sun in the east are stronger than when they set after the Sun in the west: "The positions of planets oriental of the Sun ... signify a temperament that is liberal, unaffected, pleasant, strong, ingenious, quick thinking, and open ... the vespertine rising of the planets,

especially those posited in the 7th House, signifies a temperament that is unstable, weak, intolerant of work, prone to sudden affections, litigious, and troubled in marriage." [Morinus Book 18, page 47]. Also, in Book 21 he states that: "Observe (a planet's) position in relation to the Sun and the Moon, for oriental to the Sun and above the earth during the day, and similarly, occidental to the Moon, are more effective and bring forth more striking results; in the contrary positions planets are weaker and their action more obscure." [Morinus Book 21, page 91].

However my own work with the inner planets Mercury and Venus contradicts this: when oriental (rising in the east before the Sun) the inner planets act in a different manner than when occidental (setting in the west after the Sun), but it is not correct to say that one mode is stronger than the other. In this I agree with Morinus, rather than Jerome Cardan (Cardanus), who states that "Cardan (in his Commentary on text 14, Chapter 3 of Book 2 of the Quadripartite) is of the opinion that because an oriental planet has so different a valence [value] than when that same planet is occidental, it behaves as if it were not a single planet but rather [acts] like two completely different planets. Such a proposition is false because in both states [oriental or occidental] the planet acts according to its own inner nature, albeit in a different mode. The nature of a planet is unique and immutable, but its modes or states are varied." [Morinus Book 18, page 46].

In my own experience the difference between oriental and occidental is not a strength factor, but merely reveals one of two different types of functioning: personal (oriental) or impersonal (occidental). For example, when Mercury is oriental, the mentality is eager, like Gemini; when Mercury is occidental, the mentality is certain, like Virgo. Similarly, when Venus is oriental the desire nature is possessive, like Taurus; when Venus is occidental the desire nature is dispassionate, like Libra. Mercury and Venus are oriental between Inferior Conjunction and Superior Conjunction with the Sun, and they are occidental between Superior Conjunction and Inferior Conjunction. Interpretations for Mercury when oriental/occidental are posted at: http://groups.yahoo.com/group/MagicalAlmanac/files/Astrology%20Articles/.

Interpretations for Venus when oriental/occidental are given in the article 'The Politics of Relationship' posted at: http://groups.yahoo.com/group/MagicalAlmanac/files/Astrology%20Articles/.

The point is that the difference between the planets Mercury and Venus when oriental or occidental is one of predilection rather strength – it's not that one state is better or stronger than the other. Presumably this holds for the other planets as well.

Although the oriental/occidental distinction is not a strength factor, greatest brilliancy (in the cases of Mercury and Venus), which is also a function of synodic phase, is most definitely a very significant strength factor. Greatest brilliancy is as important a strength factor as being stationary or unaspected are, and it carries a similar meaning: a light, joyous, playful, self-adequacy – the freest expression of the planetary principle.

Greatest Brilliancy

It's best when the inferior planets Mercury and Venus are neither too near nor too far from the Sun. The relationship between the Sun and these two planets symbolizes what has been termed the 'Inner Child'. When the inferior planets are too close to the Sun, the Inner Child is stifled and overpowered by the parent. When the inferior planets are too far from the Sun they become arrogant and heedless. But there are two phases in the synodic cycles of Mercury and Venus (that is to say, their cycles of revolution around the Sun, as observed from the earth) in which the Inner Child has fully separated from the parent, yet has a good sense of grounding and inner certainty. These positions, where the inferior planets are neither too near nor too far from the Sun (which symbolizes the parent), are the times in their synodic cycles when Mercury and Venus reach their Greatest Brilliancy – when they really shine on their own.

What is shown by the synodic cycle of Mercury is how people believe they are in the *right*. Mercury conjunction Sun natives believe they are in the right because they are playing by the rules (whatever rules they have been taught); they are faithfully carrying out directives received from on high (inculcated by their parents and society). By contrast, when Mercury is elongated from the Sun the natives believe they are right precisely because they haven't bought into what they were taught, but rather have figured out all the angles for themselves.

Venus' synodic cycle shows what people believe they *deserve*. Venus conjunction Sun natives often feel unworthy of happiness unless they can do more or be more than is humanly possible. By contrast, when Venus is elongated from the Sun the natives have no hesitation in reaching out for and grabbing whatever they want.

Thus both cases of inferior planets conjunction Sun symbolize the natives being overwhelmed by the parent; and both cases of inferior planets elongated from Sun symbolize relative freedom from parental fiat, together with a somewhat conscienceless self-interest.

Only at the Greatest Brilliancy positions of the inferior planets – when Mercury and Venus are neither too close nor too far from the Sun – is there a good symbiosis between individual freedom on the one hand, and a sense of responsibility to something greater than personal self-interest on the other. The Greatest Brilliancy phases of the inferior planets lie between Stationary Direct and Greatest Western Elongation (i.e. between zero velocity in celestial longitude at Stationary Direct and the point where the planets equal and surpass the velocity of the Sun at Greatest Western Elongation), and also between Greatest Eastern Elongation and Stationary Retrograde (i.e. between when the planets' velocity falls below that of the Sun and Retrograde Station when velocity is zero).[3]

Mercury Greatest Brilliancy
Mercury conjunction Sun can be characterized as being a controlling, emotionally repressed know-it-all. Mercury conjunction Sun types don't think things through, but make knee-jerk judgments and snap decisions based upon what they've been taught (what their parents and society expect), and then they defend them to the death forevermore.

---

3. The synodic cycles of Mercury and Venus average 116 days and 584 days, respectively. Five Venus cycles correlate very closely with eight earth years. A complete explanation of Mercury's synodic cycle in the natal, progressed, and transiting horoscopes, including tables 1900–2050 AD, appears in Bob Makransky's book *Thought Forms*. Tables of Venus' Synodic Cycle 1900–2014 AD (an Excel worksheet) is posted at: http:// groups.yahoo.com/group/MagicalAlmanac/files/Astrology%20Articles/

There's not much self-awareness or thoughtfulness here, but beaucoup bullheadedness. On the other hand, Mercury at Greatest Western or Greatest Eastern Elongation from the Sun can be characterized as being thoughtful and understanding, but flighty and not much help to anyone, least of all themselves. Elongation types can see other people's viewpoints clearly, but are too worried and full of second thoughts to take a firm position or to stand up for themselves.

In contrast to the types in which the Mercury is either too near or too far from the Sun (the parent's influence) for its own good, the points of Greatest Brilliancy in Mercury's synodic cycle exhibit a 'just right' separation between mind and intent. Greatest Brilliancy are the only phases in Mercury's synodic cycle in which there is no great sense of personal stake in being right all the time – in particular, caring what other people think of them.

With Mercury at Greatest Brilliancy you are humble, plainspoken, and unprepossessing. Probably you feel yourself to be a misfit (at least when you were still young). There is often some sense of psychological disadvantage or handicap which you had to overcome early on, and the effort required equips you to use your experience as a teacher. You come to cherish life in itself; to treat it (and the people around you) with delicacy and restraint. You manage to find a level of being on which you can live comfortably with yourself, strike an easy, relaxed pace in life, be willing to compromise and live in peace with other people (rather than project your own inner turmoil onto them). You are perhaps the best communicator of all, even though no one understands you, because you put everything on a basis of good common sense – i.e. good faith. You are candid, reasonable, open, and straightforward. Nonetheless, you Mercury Greatest Brilliancy natives can be the most stubborn types of all; you will never act against your principles, whereas all the other Mercury cycle types can be made to back down. You no longer have the vigor to be constantly pushing yourself forward, thus you may appear to others to lack worldly ambition. You may project an image something like a sad sack or waif. To natives of the more aggressive Mercury phases you may seem wishy-washy; an ineffectual oddball whom the world is passing by. There is an ineffable sadness about Mercury Greatest Brilliancy natives, but also a heartfelt sincerity. These are the most reflective phases; the ones which most thoroughly digest and internalize their experience and the least susceptible to being fooled by superficial appearances. The highest degree of intelligence is manifested at Mercury's Greatest Brilliancy.

Venus Greatest Brilliancy
Venus conjunction Sun can be characterized as being insecure, victimized and victimizing. Venus conjunction Sun types define themselves – and let their self-esteem depend – on some impossible ideal they have of themselves. They can be overly clingy and smothery; they will nourish and protect dependents, but will not permit themselves to become emotionally dependent on anyone. They feel a constant need to be proving their worth, and tend to find relationships frustrating and disillusioning. On the other hand, Venus at Greatest Western or Greatest Eastern Elongation from the Sun can be characterized as being cold, remote and manipulative. Unlike the introspective conjunction types who feel ashamed of being too happy, Venus elongation types will instinctively move to dominate situations and relationships and get whatever it is they want from others, one way or another. Their empire-building is best described by the adjectives cool, efficient, and pragmatic.

In contrast to the types in which the Venus is either too near or too far from the Sun (the parent's approval) for its own good, the phases of Greatest Brilliancy in Venus' synodic cycle exhibit a 'just right' separation between desire and intent. When Venus is at its Greatest Brilliancy (which is exact at an elongation of about 39° from the Sun, roughly 36 days before and after Inferior Conjunction), you possess an easy manner which puts other people at their ease as well. You are untroubled and unhurried. Your genius lies in your ability to take things as they come, to adapt to your environment and other people rather than to bend them and yourself out of shape; effortless self-application. In contrast to the Venus conjunction types you have little need for the hallmark of earnest striving in all that you do to validate your expenditure. You have a stress-free manner, a sense of being completely relaxed and comfortable – of having made your peace with yourself. You know your own worth and are aware of your limitations; you make no apologies for yourself, and you try to expect the best in others. Your sense of self-esteem and self-worth arise from within; they are not determined by what other people think of you. Because you have so little dependence on outside feedback you can be unduly cocksure, imperious, and unquestioning of your own motives. When Venus Greatest Brilliancy natives are scoundrels (which can happen, depending upon what's going on in the rest of the chart) they make excellent confidence men since everyone trusts them implicitly. You possess an emotional economy which, in true Marxist fashion, takes only what it needs and gives out whatever it is capable of.

The Fixed Stars

"Not only are conjunctions between planets and fixed stars of the first magnitude efficacious, but also effective are the aspects between them, at least the major and partile ones, since the fixed stars have their own movement through the signs of the zodiac as do the planets. This is true not only of the fixed stars that lie near the Ecliptic, but also of those that are more distant (from the Ecliptic)". [Morinus Book 18, page 66].

"Observe which of the fixed stars are conjunct the planet, or with which one does rise, culminate, or set; for the brightest stars produce important and unexpected effects, as experience frequently makes clear." [Morinus Book 21, page 92].

The strength conferred by a bright star conjunct a planet in your horoscope shows a place of protection, a safe haven in your chart. Bright stars show in what areas of life and in what ways you can proceed at your own pace and pursue your own aims, unimpeded and unthreatened. Even when a star has a nominally malefic meaning, nonetheless when it conjoins a natal planet it means protection, although in this case the protection will be a matter of closing up into oneself instead of reaching out to others (which is how the benefic stars operate through the planets they conjoin). Conjunction with any bright star, whether nominally benefic or malefic, must be deemed to be a powerful strength factor in a natal horoscope because it symbolizes an easy adjustment to the indicated situations; which in turn tends to encourage or draw easy circumstances.

Exactly which areas of life are affected depend upon the planets and houses involved. For example, Prince Charles's Sun conjoins the star

Agena on the 5th cusp (children, sports, love affairs), so these are the areas of the Prince's life where his **purpose** is liberated, adventurous, idealistic, experimental, young (i.e. protected). Similarly, planets conjunct bright stars in the 2nd house grant a facility for dealing with money matters (such as the Jupiter-Pluto conjunction on Regulus in the 2nd house of Bill Gates' chart); in the 10th house they make for a natural leadership ability and sense of group responsibility (such as the Uranus conjunction with Pollux on Mohandas Ghandi's MC) and so forth.

The manner in which the benefic influence of the bright stars differs from the benefic influence of – for example – the angles, North Node, Part of Fortune, Venus, or Jupiter is that these other benefic points are not so much places of protection as of opportunity. They don't shield us from the buffeting of circumstances so much as they give us some sort of advantage in coming to grips with them. Where these points fall (if they are well-aspected in the natal chart) we get our lucky breaks in life.

By contrast, conjunction with a bright star is not so much a matter of increased luck as it is a matter of repose, ease, self-adequacy and insulation from the cycle of rewards and punishments which drives most of our everyday existence. Conjunction with a bright star endows a planet with a sense of refinement, ultimacy, art-for-art's-sake.

If this description sounds vague, it's because the bright stars themselves vary considerably in their individual meanings. Some stars are benefic in influence, while others are decidedly malefic. However, even stars which normally produce unhappy events by primary direction must be considered to elevate the action of planets they conjoin in the natal chart, since they expand the scope of the planets outside the humdrum routine of everyday life, and focus the planetary energies on higher, more abstract designs.

I suggest using orbs no greater than one degree for conjunctions with fixed stars, and, to gainsay Morinus' suggestion (in the quotation at the beginning of this section), to use only conjunctions (not other aspects). Since several pairs of bright stars are located very close together (in longitude that is – they're widely separated in the sky), it is suggested that conjunctions to Sirius, Spica and Fomalhaut only be considered when the planets involved occupy longitudes *less* than these stars, and that conjunctions to Canopus, Arcturus and Deneb only be considered when the planets involved occupy longitudes *greater* than these stars. That way we can more easily separate out the individual meanings of Sirius versus Canopus, Spica versus Arcturus, and Fomalhaut versus Deneb.

Some of the work I have done with conjunctions of natal planets to fixed stars indicates that Morinus' view expressed in the quotation at the beginning of this section is quite correct: conjunctions of planets to fixed stars in Right Ascension (so that the planets culminate at the same moment as the stars) and Oblique Ascension (so that the planets rise at the same moment as the stars) are as efficacious as conjunctions in longitude; moreover the three measures have somewhat different flavors.

Tables of positions and interpretations for the 20 brightest stars (all stars brighter than magnitude 1.5) are given below. Note that precession moves the stars forward in the zodiac at a rate of .014 degrees per year. The 'Radix' entry for each star is a list of ideas associated with that star when it is found within one degree of conjunction with a planet in the horoscope. The 'By Direction' entry lists the kinds of events which might be expected in the month or two *following* the conjunction of a bright star with an angle by primary direction. For instructions on how to calculate these directions see my free downloadable *Primary Directions* book posted at: http://www.dearbrutus.com/buyprimarydirections.html. Tables of the 137 brightest stars (all stars brighter than magnitude 3) are also included in this book.

Table of the Twenty Brightest Stars

(Longitudes of stars brighter than magnitude 1.5 as of January 1st of given year. The second column of the table shows the planet whose influence the star most nearly resembles, per Makransky. The third column is the Bayer designation of the star.)

Star	Nature	Bayer	1900	1920	1940	1960	1980	2000
Aldebaran	SA	α Tau	8GE23	8GE40	8GE57	9GE13	9GE30	9GE47
Rigel	ME	β Ori	15GE26	15GE42	15GE59	16GE16	16GE32	16GE49
Capella	VE	α Aur	20GE27	20GE44	21GE01	21GE17	21GE34	21GE51
Betelgeuze	SU	α Ori	27GE21	27GE38	27GE55	28GE11	28GE28	28GE45
Sirius	ME	α CMa	12CN42	12CN58	13CN15	13CN31	13CN48	14CN05
Canopus	SA	α Car	13CN35	13CN51	14CN08	14CN24	14CN40	14CN57
Pollux	ME	β Gem	21CN50	22CN06	22CN23	22CN39	22CN56	23CN13
Procyon	MO	α CMi	24CN24	24CN41	24CN57	25CN14	25CN30	25CN47
Regulus	SU	α Leo	28LE26	28LE43	28LE59	29LE16	29LE32	29LE49
Spica	SA	α Vir	22LI27	22LI43	23LI00	23LI16	23LI33	23LI50
Arcturus	MA	α Boo	22LI50	23LI07	23LI23	23LI40	23LI57	24LI13
Mimosa	SA	β Cru	10SC15	10SC32	10SC49	11SC05	11SC21	11SC38
Agena	MA	β Cen	22SC24	22SC41	22SC57	23SC14	23SC30	23SC47
Bungula	VE	α Cen	28SC12	28SC28	28SC44	29SC00	29SC16	29SC32
Antares	MA	α Sco	8SG22	8SG38	8SG55	9SG12	9SG28	9SG45
Vega	ME	α Lyr	13CP55	14CP11	14CP28	14CP45	15CP02	15CP19
Altair	JU	α Aql	0AQ22	0AQ39	0AQ55	1AQ12	1AQ29	1AQ46
Fomalhaut	SU	α PsA	2PI27	2PI44	3PI01	3PI17	3PI34	3PI51
Deneb	ME	α Cyg	3PI57	4PI13	4PI30	4PI46	5PI03	5PI19
Achernar	MA	α Eri	13PI53	14PI10	14PI27	14PI44	15PI01	15PI18

Star	Nature	Bayer	2020	2040	2060	2080	2100	2120
Aldebaran	SA	α Tau	10GE03	10GE20	10GE37	10GE54	11GE11	11GE28
Rigel	ME	β Ori	17GE06	17GE23	17GE39	17GE56	18GE13	18GE30
Capella	VE	α Aur	22GE07	22GE24	22GE41	22GE58	23GE15	23GE32
Betelgeuze	SU	α Ori	29GE01	29GE18	29GE35	29GE52	0CN09	0CN26
Sirius	ME	α CMa	14CN21	14CN37	14CN54	15CN10	15CN27	15CN44
Canopus	SA	α Car	15CN13	15CN30	15CN47	16CN03	16CN20	16CN37
Pollux	ME	β Gem	23CN29	23CN45	24CN02	24CN19	24CN35	24CN52
Procyon	MO	α CMi	26CN03	26CN19	26CN36	26CN53	27CN10	27CN26
Regulus	SU	α Leo	0VI06	0VI22	0VI39	0VI56	1VI13	1VI30
Spica	SA	α Vir	24LI06	24LI23	24LI40	24LI57	25LI14	25LI31
Arcturus	MA	α Boo	24LI30	24LI47	25LI04	25LI20	25LI37	25LI54
Mimosa	SA	β Cru	11SC55	12SC11	12SC28	12SC45	13SC01	13SC18
Agena	MA	β Cen	24SC03	24SC20	24SC37	24SC54	25SC10	25SC27
Bungula	VE	α Cen	29SC43	29SC58	0SG13	0SG28	0SG44	0SG59
Antares	MA	α Sco	10SG02	10SG18	10SG35	10SG52	11SG09	11SG26
Vega	ME	α Lyr	15CP35	15CP52	16CP09	16CP26	16CP43	17CP00
Altair	JU	α Aql	2AQ03	2AQ20	2AQ37	2AQ54	3AQ11	3AQ28
Fomalhaut	SU	α PsA	4PI08	4PI25	4PI42	4PI59	5PI16	5PI33
Deneb	ME	α Cyg	5PI35	5PI52	6PI09	6PI25	6PI42	6PI59
Achernar	MA	α Eri	15PI35	15PI52	16PI09	16PI26	16PI44	17PI01

Bright Fixed Star Interpretations

Aldebaran
Nature of Saturn. *Radix*: benevolent, self-contained, mannerly, punctilious, reasonable, intellectually curious, cool, competent, steadfast. *By Direction*: Helplessness, oppression; circumstances beyond one's personal control.

Rigel
Nature of Mercury. *Radix*: Dreamy, aloof, preoccupied, optimistic, self-motivated, outspoken, brash, acerbic, sassy. *By Direction*: Enthusiasm; birth of new skills and interests.

Capella
Nature of Venus. *Radix*: Refined sensibilities, aesthetic (effete); dilettante; maintains own space and distance; prefers solitude (above-it-all, snooty). *By Direction*: Emotional turmoil, sticky entanglements with others.

Betelgeuze
Nature of the Sun. *Radix*: Easygoing, sociable, gregarious, alert, ironic, sardonic, entertaining, earnest, upright; intent and determined without making waves. *By Direction*: Pause for reflection; shed illusions and face reality.

Sirius
Nature of Mercury. *Radix*: Sociable, conversational, makes a good impression, deft at handling people, businesslike, well-organized, in-charge (impatient, stickler for details). *By Direction*: Turning over a new leaf; starting a new life or career.

Canopus
Nature of Saturn. *Radix*: Serious, morose, pessimistic, critical, cynical, heavyweight. *By Direction*: Limitation, restriction, heavy emotional pressure; imposed upon by others; anguish.

Pollux
Nature of Mercury. *Radix*: Fresh, naive, impetuous, exuberant, open, analytical, curious. *By Direction*: New worlds to conquer; new perspectives and responsibilities; coming into one's own.

Procyon
Nature of the Moon. *Radix*: Emotionally centered, in touch with innermost feelings, cautious, shrewd, independent, aloof; unflagging hopefulness, faith and endurance. *By Direction*: Intense, emotional; things come to a head; calls for hard work and dedicated effort.

Regulus
Nature of the Sun. *Radix*: Proud, dignified, regal bearing, grand manner (expects to be served), genial, unvarnished, unabashed. *By Direction*: Power, prowess, exuberance; take control of life.

Spica
Nature of Saturn. *Radix*: Sincere, determined, inner strength, courage, stiff upper lip, obstinate (easily put-upon, autocratic). *By Direction*: Heavy pressure; difficulties with others; deception or underhandedness; strange, worrisome undercurrents.

Arcturus
Nature of Mars. *Radix*: Friendly, up-front, outgoing, natural, unaffected, candid, childlike, mischievous, daring, *joie de vivre*. *By Direction*: Ambition, self-respect; new opportunities and friendships.

Mimosa
Nature of Saturn. *Radix*: Calm, self-possessed, unhurried, dignified, self-controlled, idealistic, attuned to nuances (stubborn, haughty). *By Direction*: Need to triumph over adversity; stand up for oneself.

Agena
Nature of Mars. *Radix*: Idealistic, romantic, mystical, adventurous, liberated (aloof, touchy). *By Direction*: Release from pressure and uncertainty; new direction in life.

Bungula
Nature of Venus. *Radix*: Abstracted, otherworldly, on own wavelength, optimistic, hopeful, vulnerable, childlike, gentle and genteel. *By Direction*: Move or journey; search for a more congenial environment.

Antares
Nature of Mars. *Radix*: Cocky, brash, outspoken, bull-headed, acute, humorous (caustic), unflagging energy and optimism. *By Direction*: 'Coming home', finding one's niche, where one belongs.

Vega
Nature of Mercury. *Radix*: Eager, animated, outgoing, bubbly, sunny disposition and cheerful attitude. *By Direction*: Freedom, independence; take control of own affairs.

Altair
Nature of Jupiter. *Radix*: Laconic, frank, plain-spoken, benevolent, optimistic, humorous, mischievous, rebellious. *By Direction*: Escape from a rut; new outlook, interests, and hope.

Fomalhaut
Nature of the Sun. *Radix*: No-nonsense, down-to earth, meticulous, practical, honorable, idealistic, lofty (proud, authoritarian). *By Direction*: Move or career change; new responsibilities, new horizons.

Deneb
Nature of Mercury. *Radix*: Open, vivacious, intellectually curious, nonjudgmental, courageous; unflinching readiness to stand up for beliefs. *By Direction*: After a frustrating period, one embarks upon new ventures and relationships.

Achernar
Nature of Mars. *Radix*: Stubborn, determined, single-minded, responsible, hardworking (pig-headed, dictatorial), daring, cheeky, independent in thought and action. *By Direction*: Difficult adjustments; emotional pressure; jealousy.

Appendix 1: The Local Determination

The Ascendant: its Aspects-Ruler-Occupants

"The ruler of the Ascendant applying to the Sun, which is always analogous to honors, indicates honors for the native; when applying to Jupiter, which is analogous to money it indicates wealth; when applying to Venus, which is analogous to a wife, it indicates the wife when Venus is in the seventh house or ruler of the seventh. And so, careful attention should be paid to the planets' location and house, or their house rulerships, and to whether they aspect favorably or unfavorably a planet having an analogy with the meanings of these houses, and what the celestial state and determinations of this other planet may in turn be. From all this a very accurate prognostication can be made, for herein lie the secrets of astrology." [Morinus Book 21, page 14].

Traditionally, the first house of the horoscope and particularly the rising degree are said to represent the personality. This is one of those wonderful astrological aphorisms which don't mean anything, since it's equally true to say that the horoscope in its entirety represents the personality. In what sense, then, can it be said that the first house symbolizes the personality? And what distinct aspects of personality are symbolized by the components of the first house – the rising degree, the ruling planet, and the planet(s) occupying the first house?

In answer to the second question, at least, we will say that the occupants of the first house symbolize the inner personality, which operates on a level of feeling. That is to say, planets in the first house symbolize the natives' striving side, their urge to be somebody. The Ascendant ruler (i.e. the planet which rules the sign on the cusp of the first house) symbolizes the outer personality or self-projection, which operates on a level of mind – that is, the natives' superficial manner and mannerisms. The rising degree symbolizes the social and psychological milieu in which the natives operate (acceptance or rejection) as well as their adaptation to it – that is, the rose petals or brickbats they find being hurled at them from the sidelines.

We can get at the differences between these three aspects of personality by contrasting their operation within the horoscope, but first we'll need some preliminary definitions.

All aspects are taken with six-degree orbs. The occupants of the first house are those planets which lie between 5° above the Ascendant and 5° above the 2nd house cusp.[1] The Ascendant ruler is the planet ruling the sign on the first house cusp; Uranus, Neptune, and Pluto will not be considered to rule any signs.

The rising degree is the native's point of entrance into the mundane sphere, the matrix of his or her personality, and as such it symbolizes how people make a place for themselves in the world, and how the world in turn receives them. The focus here is not so much on the natives themselves as on the space they take up, on the way in which their environment bends itself around them and how they must bend themselves to fit into it.

"The degree of the sign rising has greater significance for the native than the ruler of the Ascendant or a planet in the first house." [Morinus Book 21, page 21].

The aspects which the rising degree receives show where the natives are able to make easy adjustments to their social environment, and where they must struggle to conform to the expectations of others. The fact that the houses which symbolize the parents (fourth and tenth) square the ascendant, and the house of the partner (seventh) opposes it, shows that these are the relationships which are intrinsically problematical; similarly the houses of the children (fifth), friends (eleventh), and siblings (third) symbolize relationships which are intrinsically helpful or joyous. But in the individual case much depends upon which houses are actually occupied, and by which planets. For example, the Sun square the rising degree may mean rejection by the father even if the Sun is not in the fourth house. (Morinus would disagree with this proposition).

When your **Ascendant** (rising degree) **is well-aspected**, you are accepted by other people more or less on your own terms. You have

---

1. This is not the place to delve into the house division question.

a cool, detached manner which enables you to move deftly through other people without banging into them. You have a facility for being impersonal and brusque without stirring antagonism. You slide easily into social situations; you have a sense of *noblesse oblige* or divine right with which you take your place in the midst of your fellows and command their respect.

When your **Ascendant is afflicted**, you generally feel misunderstood or unappreciated. It is difficult for you to find your niche because you feel that everyone's eye is on you. Your outreach misses its mark because you look outward towards what you think is acceptable, or to whom you think you ought to be, rather than inward to who you really are. You are constantly having to give ground or compromise yourself, alternately tiptoeing around people or else overstepping yourself and stomping on them. You find it hard to accept yourself, hence you make it hard for other people to accept you in turn.

The ruling planet represents the native's outer personality, the role or persona adopted in casual social transactions: "When the Lord of the figure of a Nativity shall be Retrograde, and both ways Cadent; the Native will be a weak, poor-spirited, dejected fellow, bringing nothing to perfection." [Jerome Cardan, *Seven Segments*].

When your **Ascendant Ruler is retrograde** your outer personality – your manner and style – is especially quixotic. In one fashion or another you represent an extreme human type – a caricature of normality. You must live up to something: you proudly uphold some standard of human conduct, and you play your chosen life role more conscientiously than most people do. You are truly an original, a memorable character. You are fussy and detailed, and you have to have everything just so. You live in a busyness, a flurry of activity, without seeming to get anywhere in particular. You are sustained by a deeply felt *joie de vivre*; even at those times of powerlessness and helplessness when you retreat into your black moods of self-pity you never lose your doughty mettle and irrepressibility.

When your **Ascendant Ruler is stationary** you possess the same hearty and vivacious manner as the retrograde type, and you are equally diligent and high-principled. However, you are more discriminating and prudent – not so much modest as circumspect. You take on a parental or avuncular persona, and you show a friendly (albeit detached) interest in other people. Thus you maintain your own balance and keep yourself on a more even emotional keel than the self-obsessed retrograde type.

The essential dignity or debility of the ruling planet shows the native's style of conduct – whether you are vigorous or gentle, and the aspects which the ruling planet receives show the native's everyday attitude – whether you are optimistic or pessimistic.

When your **Ascendant Ruler is in good celestial state**, your ego is in robust condition. You are a tough-charger, bold and brassy, with considerable panache and pizzazz. You have a single-minded determination which plows right on ahead and doesn't look back. When you talk to people, it is as though you were holding forth to a rapt audience, with a knowing 'How'm I doing?' look in your eye. You have a snappy, face-front, chest-out style – bright-eyed, bushy-tailed, and ready for action.

When your **Ascendant Ruler is in bad celestial state**, you are simple and plain-spoken, and try to keep yourself in the background. You are a shrinking violet, enveloped in a miasma of burden or onus, as if you were carrying the whole world's problems on your shoulders. There is a sense of effeteness about you – you seem to heave a sigh with every breath. You are compliant and self-effacing, with a subdued, almost apologetic 'aw shucks' kind of style.

When your **Ascendant Ruler is unaspected**, you are plain-spoken and plain-dealing, with a down-home, 'aw shucks' kind of style. While no one is going to call you self-effacing – indeed you are regarded as quite a character – nevertheless your self-promotion is sufficiently laid-back and low-key that other people find your presence soothing and refreshing rather than stimulating or jarring, as with aspected Ascendant rulers. Thus you are able to manage other people smoothly by adapting yourself to them or being ruthless with them, as need be, without feeling that you are being forced, put upon, or bent out of shape. You know when it's time to call a spade a spade, and you also know when to set aside the postures and attitudinizing in order to tune into a wavelength of understanding and compassion.

When your **Ascendant Ruler is well-aspected**, you adopt an everyday attitude of expansive optimism and good cheer. There is a good-natured ostentation or presumptuousness about you which is prepossessing rather than offensive. You have an impish irreverence, and you know exactly what you can get away with. You use your cockiness and archness to gloss over serious difficulties and to minimize serious problems. You come on like an emcee or social director: "Is everybody happy?!"

When your **Ascendant Ruler is afflicted**, you adopt a somber or pessimistic everyday attitude. You tend to be guarded, mistrustful, and suspicious of people and their motives. You hold yourself back with people, are coy, and have to be drawn out of your shell. You are alternately stiff and defensive, or else dissident and pugnacious. There may be an intolerant, absolutist streak in you, and a fondness for contention. You generally expect the worst and are overjoyed when it happens: "Aha! I told you so!"

We can observe the difference between essential dignity and dignity by being well-aspected more clearly by contrasting the two extreme cases:

When your **Ascendant Ruler is in good celestial state but afflicted**, you are an outspoken pessimist. You are a perennial cynic, with an ironic sense of humor and a rather low opinion of your fellow bipeds. You enjoy being perverse and contrary just for the hell of it, and you are always ready with a sardonic comment to fit any occasion.

When your **Ascendant Ruler is well-aspected but in bad celestial state**, you are a subdued optimist. You are genial and unassuming, generally solicitous and sympathetic to others. You possess a strong sense of balance or proportion, and you don't offer counsel so much as try to be open and supportive, and to look at the bright side of things: "Cheer up, old fellow!"

"When the Lord of the Mid-heaven separates by Retrogradation from the Lord of the Ascendant, the Prince, King, or Ruler, shall be averse to the Native, but if on the other side the Lord of the Ascendant being Retrograde forsakes the Lord of the tenth, then the Native shall hate his Prince, King, or Governors; the like is to be understood of other houses according to their respective significations.

"When the Lord of the second applies to the Lord of the Ascendant; especially if that Lord of the Ascendant be Jupiter; the Native shall, all his life time, be happy in acquiring riches even to admiration.

"When the Lord of the Ascendant beholds the Sun with a friendly aspect or is Oriental next to the Sun, or joined with the

Lord of the tenth, the Native will be much beloved by Kings and great people; for the cause of which favour consider the nature of the said Lord of the Ascendant and his place." [Jerome Cardan, *Seven Segments*].

The aspects between the ruling planet and the rising degree describe the symbiosis or antagonism between your superficial role and your inner sense of who you want to be.

When your **Ascendant Ruler well-aspects the rising degree**, you are calm and self-assured in a social situation. You neither shrink from the limelight, nor do you hasten to push yourself into it. You are a patient and sympathetic listener, and an apt and pithy interlocutor. You consider conversation to be a dialogue, and enjoyable opportunity to share ideas and feelings.

When your **Ascendant Ruler afflicts the rising degree**, you are tense and uncomfortable in a social situation. You alternate between being overly hesitant and tongue-tied, and overly demonstrative or abrupt. Your remarks are often out of place or jarring to other people since you take conversation as if it were an interview in which you are being judged.

Every horoscope has a rising degree and a ruler, but not every horoscope has an occupied first house. With the occupants of the first house we come to a deeper level of personality than that shown by the rising degree or ruler. This may be termed the inner personality, your sense of security or centeredness within yourself. Where the ruling planet represents the face you show to others, the occupants of the first house represent what you see in your mirror.

When your **first house is unoccupied**, your personality is not such a problem or an issue in your life. You are matter-of-fact and unselfconscious. You take yourself for granted – i.e. you feel no great need to be constantly justifying or proving yourself to anyone.

When your first house is occupied by a planet or planets, personality is indeed an issue for you. The more planets in your first house, the more self-conscious and self justifying you are, and the more intensely you feel that you must assert yourself to be someone of importance.

When **the occupants of your first house are in good celestial state**, you have a high opinion of yourself and your own capabilities *vis-à-*

vis other people. You are more conscientious or overreaching than is expected or even necessary; you feel a strong need to outdo other people, and even yourself. You mantle yourself in a fierce independence of spirit and a sense of superiority.

When **the occupants of your first house are in bad celestial state**, you see yourself as placed at a disadvantage *vis-á-vis* other people in the race of life; hence, you don't even make the effort to outshine them. You really don't like being the focus of attention, and are quite willing to play second fiddle and let the glory go to others. You take your satisfaction in plodding along at your own unhurried pace.

When **the occupants of your first house are well-aspected**, you tend to be overly pleased with yourself. The reactions other people have to you, whether positive or negative, tend only to confirm your own irreproachability and virtuosity. You put on an easy-going front, unhurried and unruffled, and you are rather disdainful of other people's clamor. "What's your problem?"; "What's your hurry?" are your standard responses to any criticism or exigency.

When **the occupants of your first house are afflicted**, you tend to be overly exacting with yourself. The reactions other people have to you make you bristle and take a fighting stance, as if to say: "Who the hell are you to be judging me?" You tend to be easily bothered or annoyed, and even positive feedback puts you out: "No, no, that isn't what I meant!" You protect your thin skin by putting on a front of tough, hardnosed determination.

We can differentiate between the essential dignity and the dignity by aspect of the first-house occupants by contrasting the two extreme cases.

When **the occupants of your first house are in good celestial state but afflicted**, you are proud but touchy. You like to think that you are above it all, but you are more sensitive to negative feedback than you will let on, even to yourself. You have lofty ambitions and ideals, but inhibit yourself by a deep-seated fear of censure.

When **the occupants of the first house are well-aspected but in bad celestial state**, you are unambitious but smug. You are circumscribed in your outlook, but within your sphere of operation you won't be budged or moved, or even listen to reason. You set your sights low, but then expect to be left alone, in peace, to go your way unmolested.

The aspects between the ruling planet and the occupants of the first house describe the symbiosis or antagonism between your superficial role and your inner sense of who you want to be.

When your **Ascendant Ruler well-aspects the occupants of your first house,** you possess a convincing ease and simplicity of manner. You are candid and straightforward in your dealings with others; you don't put on airs or make an effort to impress. You are willing to share even your deepest feelings with unapologetic sincerity. You are childlike in your naiveté and guilelessness, and in your spontaneous enthusiasm and alacrity.

When your **Ascendant Ruler afflicts the occupants of your first house,** there is often a deep breach between your cool and self-assured outer manner and your need for warmth and understanding. You feel you have to live up to an idealized image you have of yourself, and thus you don't allow yourself much latitude to express your deeper feelings and doubts. You won't permit yourself to show any cracks in your polished facade, nor will you ever admit weakness or fear, even to yourself. The greater your pain, the more you congeal into the Great Stone Face.

The Descendant: its Aspects-Ruler-Occupants

If an astrologer predicts "serious difficulties in partnership," there's a 99% chance that he or she is right without even needing to look at the horoscope. What the horoscope (and in particular the 7th house) shows is not how smooth and tranquil your partnerships will be (which is more a matter of Venus and her aspectual state), but rather what it is you are seeking in partnership – the kind of relationship and partner you want.

The Ascendant (1st house) shows how you present yourself to the world: go out on the worldly stage to do your act, take your bows, receive applause (or criticism, as the case may be). By contrast, the Descendant (7th house) shows a deeper aspect of yourself, in which you hunker down, take and defend a position, meet other people eyeball-to-eyeball.

Where the 1st house shows your surface, outward personality, the 7th house shows where you must dig in your heels, define the limits of your personal space through trade-offs, compromise, hard bargaining. The 'living happily ever after' image prevalent in our society is a falsehood: a successful partnership always requires hard, dedicated work and constant vigilance.

The condition of the Descendant and 7th house in your natal chart shows your general approach to intimate relationships with equals – your partnership style – not how happy or successful these relationships will be. Prognostication of personal happiness (or its lack) is made basically from the condition of the planet Venus: Venus strong by sign and aspect shows a person who has a strong ego and sense of self-worth, who has no hesitation in reaching out and taking what he or she wants from life. A weak Venus shows a timid person with low self-esteem, whose outreach tends to fall short of the mark (since he or she may feel undeserving of happiness). Strong Venus = fulfillment mode, and weak Venus = denial mode.

The point is that what is shown by the 7th house is your approach to the institution of partnership (which means business as well as marital partnerships) rather than how successful you will be at making this institution into something joyous and fulfilling in your own life.

As Noel Tyl points out, the 7th house invariably opposes the 1st; that is to say, partnership is fundamentally a matter of combat (opposition), not collaboration (as are the sextile and trine relationships – friends, siblings, children, grandparents – shown by the 11th, 3rd, 5th and 9th houses). For example, even when the 7th house cusp, the ruling planet of the 7th, and the planetary occupants of the 7th are all well-aspected, this does not guarantee a happy partnership (nor do all three afflicted forbid one).

The Descendant, ruler and occupants all well-aspected merely means that for you partnership must be a convenience, or nothing. You choose a partner like a consumer chooses a product – you enter into partnership in order to advance conscious goals rather than as an *affaire d'amour* or something to sweat and bleed over. You don't let yourself get into a tizzy about partnership (which can actually be a source of problems if seen by your partner as a lack of interest and commitment).

The Descendant (the point in the zodiac setting at the time of your birth), together with the aspects made to it, symbolize your personal adaptation to society's definition of partnership –how lightly or heavily the mantle of 'spouse' sits upon your shoulders. The focus is on you as an individual relating to the institution of partnership as an abstraction.

The ruler of the 7th house (the planet which rules the sign on the Descendant) shows your superficial role-playing *vis-a-vis* partnership: what you assume your partner will be or do for you. The focus is on your expectations and images of your partner (i.e. the part of yourself you feel is 'missing' and want a partner to supply for you).

The occupants of the 7th house symbolize your actual, flesh-and-blood partner(s) – not what you wish for (shown by the ruler), but what you get (the realities you must deal with in partnership). For example, Sun in the 7th shows a powerful, dominating, independent partner, who will challenge your own self-possession and sense of mastery. Any planets occupying the 7th house symbolize issues of control and manipulation.

Descendant unaspected (which implies Ascendant unaspected as well): You are basically a loner – outspoken, unconventional, on your own wavelength, and not in synch with the people around you. You march to the beat of a distant drum, don't fit it or play the social game by the usual rules. You feel separated from others by a chasm of *Angst*; you are consciously aware of your aloneness (which most people cover up with superficial socializing).

Descendant well-aspected: You have an easy, take-it-or-leave-it approach to partnership. You take conflicts in stride, refuse to allow intimate relationships to become stressful or cause inner turmoil. You maintain a light touch, a respectful distance, and refuse to be intruded or imposed upon (which your partner may see as a refusal to take his or her feelings seriously).

Descendant afflicted: (note that planets conjunct the Ascendant will oppose the Descendant – i.e. the same strategies, postures, and come-ons that are so effective in winning over casual acquaintances, will be the very attitudes and actions that produce stress and conflict in intimate relationships. Intimates can't be wowed or wooed by the superficial self-promotion which characterizes casual relationships). You tend to be passive, overly accepting and tolerant of other people's encroachments in your space. You are insecure in partnership, afraid of rejection, loath to stand up and assert yourself; at the same time you are rather clinging and possessive. There is a need here for lightening up and letting go.

Descendant ruler unaspected: You are emotionally isolated, feel little need for sharing, and hence you tend to enter into partnership either because it's the generally accepted and expected thing to do, or else for some ulterior purpose (e.g. to have children). You don't put much emotional investment into your partnerships, and therefore never lose your sense of strategic independence.

Descendant ruler well-aspected: You are breezy and self-assured in intimate relationship. You naturally expect your partner defer to you, and you can be quite bossy and insistent. But you're not overbearing or officious – rather, you just know what you want out of a partnership and you operate on the assumption that that's how it will be.

Descendant ruler afflicted: You have no clear picture of what you're doing in a partnership (or what your own needs and objectives are). You stumble into it, and stumble along thereafter. You therefore tend have feelings of disgruntlement and dissatisfaction with your current state of intimate affairs, but no motivation to take action change things to better suit yourself.

Descendant ruler in good celestial state: You have a rather naive, childlike, buoyant, optimistic approach to intimate relationships. You're like a little puppy. You love being in love, are thoughtful about the little things that make your partner happy, and try to make partnership fun and adventurous.

Descendant ruler in bad celestial state: You cultivate self-reliance, and try not to become too dependent on your partner. In all your assumptions you look towards the day when the relationship will end (as all relationships, in one fashion or another eventually must). You see partnership in terms of profit and loss, and therefore miss out on a lot of joy and spontaneity.

Descendant ruler in good aspect to Descendant: You are the one who runs your relationships – the one who calls the shots, gives the orders, makes the partnership decisions for both. You expect your partner to indulge and pamper you, and can be a bit vain or prissy – as if your partner is first and foremost your servant.

Descendant ruler afflicts Descendant: You are acquiescent in intimate relationships – you take the orders, serve your partner, let him or her make the decisions for you (so you can complain and feel put upon rather than take the responsibility for decision-making yourself).

Descendant ruler conjunct Descendant (this applies in a general way any time the ruler of the 7th house is in the 7th, even if not within orb of the descending degree): You are emotionally self-sufficient and aloof, and you seek a partner who is as strong-willed and independent as you are. Thus you either cooperate in a loose, "I do my thing and you do yours" kind of relationship, or else you lock horns with your partner, neither one ever giving an inch.

In line with the general horary[2] approach we are taking here, we consider the relationship between the rulers of the 1st and 7th houses to show how partnership serves (or hinders) the native's own self-concept and self-projection. Another way of saying this is: whether the partner bolsters or embarrasses the native in front of other people.

Descendant ruler in good aspect with Ascendant ruler: You are cheerful, optimistic and patient, and prefer to keep intimate relationships light and unruffled. You seek a partner who will accept you for yourself (on your own terms), and let you be the one who shines.

Descendant ruler afflicts Ascendant ruler: You bring a sense of guilt, inferiority, or penance to your intimate relationships. Partnership is a mirror of your shame, a reminder of how short you fall from your own image of yourself. You seek a partner with whom you can confront your doubts about your own self-worth, and need for redemption or forgiveness.

Descendant ruler conjunct Ascendant ruler: You are cool and distant, self-validating and in command of yourself and your relationships. You don't put much personal stake in partnership; you make use of it where it's helpful to you, and ignore it otherwise.

Descendant ruler disposes of Ascendant ruler (i.e. ruler of the 1st is in a sign ruled by the 7th house ruler): You're detached – not about to take any detours away from your own goals in life, nor to slow down or hurry up for anybody else. You're nonchalant and noncommittal, and you never let partnership issues bog you down or hold you back.

Ruler of 1st disposes of Descendant ruler: You put a lot of self-esteem on the line in intimate relationships (much more than you're willing to admit to yourself). You are extremely thin-skinned and easily hurt; your mood fluctuates with the acceptance or rejection you receive

---

2. In a 7th house horary question, if the Descendant ruler disposes of the Ascendant ruler, then the native (querent) is more in love with the partner than the partner is with the native; if the Ruler of the Ascendant disposes of the ruler of the Descendant, then the reverse is the case. If the two rulers are in mutual reception, then the two people are in love with one another; but in the final analysis, it is the aspect between them (whether they well-aspect or afflict one another) that determines whether the relationship will succeed or not.

from your partner, but you hide your vulnerability behind a mask of indifference and bravado.

The occupants of the 7th house (if any) describe the personality of the actual partner (or partners) – i.e. 'who' the native settles down with in the end, and the general course the relationship takes (e.g. Moon in 7th shows that partnership is never a settled, stable issue in the life, but waxes and wanes. Moon in a mutable sign in the 7th shows many partnerships).

Descendant ruler in good aspect to 7th house planets: You are bold, outspoken and brassy. Since you like to be in the limelight, you choose a partner who will hang back and play a supporting role. You are free-spirited and independent, and attract a submissive partner.

Descendant ruler afflicts 7th house planets: You are retiring in partnership and shy away from center stage. You therefore choose a partner who is outgoing, gregarious and flashy – someone who will stand up publicly (and whom you can blame; or behind whom you can hide).

No planets in 7th house: You try to avoid making issues out of partnerships; you just don't want to be bothered by it. You sidestep controversy, let things slide, and in fact will put up with considerable discomfort rather than confront relationship problems directly on your own account.

Stellium in 7th house: You possess a great openness in intimate relationship – a disarming enthusiasm and joy in sharing. You are broadminded and fair, and try to take your partner's feelings into account. You are willing to trust your partner because you trust yourself (your own motivations), and you attract a partner who is either intensely loyal, or else impossible to please (one to whom you can give your all).

Planets in 7th house well-aspected: You feel that partnership is your oyster – it's there to serve your needs. You are unabashedly manipulative and coolly matter-of-fact regarding partnership issues, and you therefore choose a partner who will come across with what's expected. If he or she doesn't, you've got the patience and cunning to outwait or outwit them.

Planets in 7th house afflicted: You see partnership as a dedication to serve others – a way of reaching out beyond yourself to do more than your share. Therefore, you choose a partner who will let you down or who won't respond to your good faith (and who will thus force you to examine your own motives).

Planets in 7th house in good celestial state: You are ardent and exuberant in intimate relationship, and love to be the leader, thus you are more calculating and controlling than sympathetic and warm. You choose a partner who will go along with you and defer to your wishes.

Planets in 7th house in bad celestial state: For you intimate relationship entails dealing with issues of your own self-worth, so you're never quite relaxed or secure with your partner. You tend to be suspicious and harbor doubts about your partner's sincerity, hence you attract a partner who will leave you feeling a bit sad or empty.

Appendix 2: Dr. Jones' Methodology

In his books (particularly *Essentials of Astrological Analysis*) Dr. Marc Edmund Jones established a framework of metasymbolism to analyze the meanings of various factors in the natal horoscope (such as retrograde planets, aspects, planets in ruler/detriment etc.). This system consists of three principles: preponderance, absence, and negative indication (which is a special case of absence).

When there is a preponderance of some factor in a natal chart (for example, a preponderance of retrograde planets, or of square aspects, or of planets conjunct critical degrees) the native's life is skewed at that point. What is shown is a weight, a self-consciousness, a sense of onus or burden, a heavy responsibility which the native must bear and bear up under. There is a depth and compulsion to act with thoroughness in this area of life, but also a heaviness and slowness. Even if the horoscope factor is nominally good, a preponderance of it becomes a source of imbalance in the life. For example, a preponderance of planets in their ruling signs comes on strong, is domineering and positive in its opinions – that is, liberates an unwieldy amount of energy and creates problems in the life.

When there is an absence of some factor in the natal horoscope, then in the area of life symbolized by that factor there is lightness, a freedom of action, and a lack of compulsion, which on the negative side can become a lack of motivation, interest, and understanding. The absence of some horoscope factor shows a freedom from responsibility, but with a concomitant lack of attunement to the environment.

The precise definition of what constitutes a 'preponderance' or 'absence' is open to adjustment depending upon the particular horoscope factor under consideration. For rare phenomena (such as stationary planets), three out of ten planets in a chart fitting the criterion is enough to constitute preponderance. Similarly, for very common phenomena (such as the presence of aspects in a horoscope, where a complete absence is unheard of), half the statistically expected number can be considered an absence. The point is that what is being shown by preponderance is a weighting in a given direction, and by absence a lack of pull in that direction.

For example, when there is a preponderance of aspects in the horoscope (at least three times as many Ptolemaic aspects as the orb in degrees – for example, at least eighteen Ptolemaic aspects within 6° orbs), the natives are critically dependent upon validation from other people for an assessment of their own worth. Since aspects are the lines that tie us to other people – compel us to seek their approval – a preponderance of aspects shows natives who are overly concerned with their images, with the impression they make on others, with being right. Therefore, they are easily bent out of shape by rejection, and they take other people's reactions too much to heart. They lack inner stability because their moods rise and fall with their current status in other people's eyes.

Conversely, an absence of aspects (less than the number of degrees in the allowable orb – that is, less than six aspects within 6° orbs) in the horoscope shows a relative freedom from worry about status in society. These natives are not particularly concerned with, motivated by, or even consciously aware of what other people think of them. They are naive and uninhibited, and say whatever's on their minds. Others accept these natives because they accept themselves, are at ease within themselves, and have a frank and natural manner. On the negative side, they can be headstrong, solipsistic, and aloof.

The third principle or metasymbolic technique for isolating the meaning of a horoscope factor is called negative indication, and it is a special form of absence. It occurs when there is a well-defined set of related horoscope factors (such as four triplicities, three quadruplicities, angular/succedent/cadent etc.) and all but one of them are represented in the natal horoscope. Whatever is symbolized by the missing factor is emphasized in a negative way – that is, as a parody, an exaggeration of the symbolism, an intellectualized, artificial version constructed as if in compensation for a felt psychological lack or need. The interpretation is similar to that of the preponderance, but with a twist: the behavior is put-on rather than heartfelt, the native acts on mind rather than on feeling.

For example, an absence of planets in fire signs makes for peppery, ornery, theatrical Prima Donnas. This is in contrast to the aristocratic bearing and quiet air of self-assurance that characterizes the preponderance of planets in fire signs. Both the preponderance and the negative indication have a manner that is competent, dominating, and superior, but the preponderance assumes it where the negative indication asserts it.

An absence of planets in earth signs makes for natives who are busy and buzzing all the time, without actually accomplishing very much. In contrast to the down-to-earth, practical self-pacing of people with a preponderance of planets in earth signs, these natives are finicky, fastidious, and never quite comfortable with things. Both the preponderance and negative indication are thorough and conscientious, but the preponderance has a clear sense of the possible (what they are comfortably capable of), whereas the negative indication is over-reaching and over-exacting of both themselves and other people.

An absence of planets in air signs makes for natives who talk a lot but don't say much of anything. Albeit sociable and gregarious, they are vague and uncommunicative on a feeling level. This contrasts with the preponderance of planets in air, which identifies people who are sharp, analytical, articulate, and tart. Both the preponderance and negative indication avidly seek relationships, but the preponderance has a clearly defined sense of who they are and what they stand for, where the negative indication is not actually comfortable with people, but go through the motions of what they feel is expected of them.

An absence of planets in water signs makes for natives who are cheerful, flighty busybodies rather than actually sympathetic or helpful to anyone. This contrasts with the sense of conscience and obligation to life which characterizes people with a preponderance of planets in water signs. Both the preponderance and negative indication are intimate, candid, and direct, but the preponderance possesses an inner dignity where the negative indication tends to be prissy and perfunctory.

These few examples illustrate the usefulness and versatility of Dr. Jones' methodology. It not only provides us with a useful investigative tool for delineating the meaning of any horoscope factor, but it also gives us a technique which can be directly applied to the interpretation of a natal horoscope.

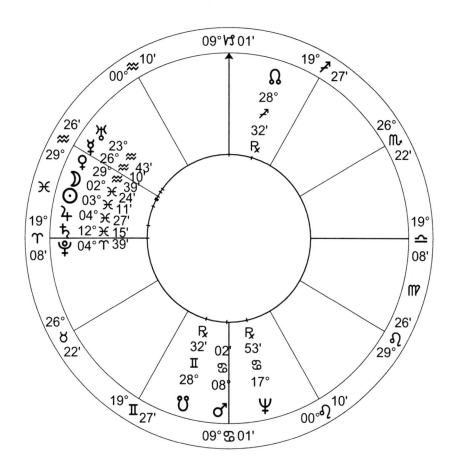

Jean-Baptiste Morin: 22 February 1583 08.33 AM LMT
Villefranche, France 45N59 04E43

Index

This index does not include references to the planets in the keywords tables; to the planets as attributes in the Fixed Stars tables; nor in the interpretations (e.g. 'Mercury Good Celestial State + Cadent' is not indexed separately under 'Mercury', 'Celestial State', or 'Cadent'), since these references are found easily enough in the main text.

5/6th 47

A

Absence 21, 48, 83, 117-119
Accidental debility ii
Accidental dignity ii
Activity xii
Afflicted ii, viii, ix, xii, 14, 21, 24, 41-49, 65, 69, 111
Air signs i, 49, 119
Angle 18, 19, 22-24, 28, 30-32, 48, 64, 74, 96, 97
  conjunction with ix, x, 3,
Angular ii, viii, x, xii-xiii, 18-24, 30-32, 41, 43, 65, 74, 118
Applying ii-iii, 47, 103, 107
Aries i, ii, v, 13
Ascendant (Asc) 18, 22, 23, 30, 32, 45, 103-110, 112, 114
Aspectual state ii, xi, xii, 41-49, 64, 69, 74, 110
Aspectual strength 41, 44, 45
Astrodynes viii
Astrolocality viii, ix
Astrologia Gallica (quotations from not separately indexed) v

B

Baldwin, Richard S. v
Book XVIII of Astrologia Gallica (quotations from not separately indexed) v

Book XXI of Astrologia Gallica (quotations from not separately indexed) v
Buddhist 41

C

Cadent ii, xii, 18-24, 65, 105, 118
Cancer ii, v, 10
Capricorn i, ii, 13
Cardan, Jerome (Cardanus) 4, 90, 105, 108
Carter, Charles 43
Celestial state i, vi, x, xii, 1-7, 22, 43, 46, 47, 64-65, 69, 103, 106
Celestial strength 18, 82
Chaplin, Charlie ii, 13
Church of Light viii
Circumstances xii
Close pairs 48
Configuration ii, 45, 47-49
Conjunction iii, 46-48, 57, 90-92, 94, 95-97
Critical degree 117

D

Debility (see Essential debility) i, ii, viii, 1, 22, 81, 82, 106
Descendant (Desc) 18, 22, 23, 30-32, 110-115
Destiny vii, viii, x
Detriment i, v, x, 3-6, 12, 69, 117
Dexter iii, 47
Dignity (see Essential dignity) i, ii, x,

1, 4-5, 12, 18, 22, 46, 48, 80, 82, 87

Dispositor (see Sole dispositor) ii, ix, 3, 4, 12-14, 46, 114

Domicile i, 2-4, 12, 46, 56, 64

E

Earth signs i, 42, 49, 119

Essential debility i, v, x, 1, 3, 4-5, 12, 106, 107, 109

Essential dignity i, v, x, 1, 3-5, 12, 106-107, 109

Exaltation sign i, ii, v, ix, x, 2-8, 20, 46

Exile i, 2, 64,

F

Fall i, x, 2-8, 69

Fan ii, 47

Feral (see Unaspected) 56

Fire signs i, 49, 118-119

Fixed stars 95-97, 100

Fixed stars, conjunction with ii, ix, 95-97; Tables 98-99

Function xii

G

Gemini v, 13, 90

Grand sextile 47

Grand square ii, 48, 49

Grand trine ii, 47, 49

Greatest brilliancy 91-95

Greatest Eastern Elongation 92-94

Greatest Western Elongation 92

H

Hindu vii

Horary 114

Horizon vi

Houses

1st ii, 2, 18, 22, 110, 114

2nd ii, 18, 46, 96, 104

3rd ii, 18, 111

4th ii, x, xi, 18

5th ii, 18, 96, 111

6th ii, 18

7th ii, x, xi, 18, 90, 110-116

8th ii, 18,

9th ii, 18, 64, 111

10th ii, 18, 22, 96

11th ii, 18, 111

12th ii, 18,

I

Imum Coeli (IC) 18, 22, 23, 30

Inferior conjunction 90, 94

Inferior planets vi, 46, 91-92

J

Jones, Dr. Marc Edmund xii, 3, 47, 117, 119

Joy i

Jupiter i, ii, v, xii, 1, 2, 13, 20, 22, 23, 45, 46, 64, 96, 103, 107

K

Karma vii, 42

Keywords xi, xii, 32

Angular Planets 33

Aspectual State 49

Celestial State 7

Stations 87

Terrestrial State 24

Kite ii, 47

L

LaBruzza, Anthony v

Leo ii, 13, 15

Libra i, v, 13, 90

Local Determination x, 47, 103-116

Longitude (celestial, or zodiacal) ii, 23, 82, 92, 96-97

M

Magnet vii

Marriage x, xi, 31, 41, 43, 90

Mars i, ii, v, xi, xii, 1, 2, 3, 10, 13, 22, 23, 41, 46

Mercury i, ii, xii, 2, 3, 13, 22, 23, 41, 46, 64, 65, 81, 82, 90, 91, 92, 93, 94

Midheaven (MC) 18, 19, 22, 23, 30, 31, 32, 96

Moon i, ii, iii, vi, xi, 2, 4, 13, 20, 22, 23, 32, 41, 45, 74, 90, 115

Morin de Villefranche, Jean Baptiste (Morinus), (other than quotations from Astrologica Gallica) i, ii, v, vi, x, xi, xii, 1-4, 46-48, 64, 80, 82, 89, 90, 96, 97, 104

Mutual reception ii, 114

N

Negative indication 117, 118-119

Neptune xii, 13, 45, 46, 82, 104

Node 46

North Node (of moon) 46, 96

O

Occidental ii, 47, 87, 89-91

Occidental astrology vi, vii, viii, 82

Occupants of 1st house 103-104, 108-110

Occupants of 7th house 110-112, 115

Opposition iii, 45, 46, 47-48, 57, 111

Orb iii, 45, 48, 49, 57, 96, 104, 113, 118

Orbit 80, 89

Oriental ii, 47, 87, 89-91, 107

P

Parallel (of declination)   56, 57

Part of Fortune 96

Partner xi, 22, 23, 31-40, 64, 104, 110-116

Peregrine i, 3, 4, 65, 69

Personality ix, x, xi, 22, 41, 56, 103-105, 108, 110, 115

Pisces ii, v

Pluto xii, 13, 22, 45, 65, 82, 96, 104

Preponderance 3, 6-7, 24, 42, 49, 58, 83, 117-119

Ptolemy i, ix, 23, 57, 89, 118

R

Rectangle ii, 47

Relationships x, xi, 10, 18, 22, 30, 31, 36, 41-45, 50, 59, 65, 74, 81, 91, 94, 104, 110- 116, 119

Retrograde vi, 80-86, 87-89, 92, 105, 106, 107, 117

Ruler
    of Ascendant 40, 103-10, 114
    of Descendant 40, 103, 110-115
    of house x, xi, 46, 103,
    of Imum Coeli (IC) 40,
    of Midheaven (MC) 40,
    of sign i, v, 2, 3, 4-6, 9, 12-13, 46, 103, 104, 117

Ruling sign i, ii, v, viii-x, 13, 20, 65, 117

S

Sagittarius i, ii

Sanchez Llacer, Pepita v

Saturn i, ii, ix, xi, xii, 1, 2, 4, 13, 22, 23, 42, 45, 46, 56, 61, 64, 65, 82

Scorpio v, 2, 13

Separating ii, iii, 45, 47, 107

Sextile iii, ix, 47, 54, 57, 62, 111

Shad Bala viii

Sidereal Zodiac v

Significator x, 22, 65, 80, 107

Sinister iii, 47

Society 14, 18, 19, 20, 30, 32, 38, 56, 57, 62, 63, 84, 91, 92, 110, 111, 118

Sole dispositor ii, ix, 12-17, 43

South Node (of moon) 46

Square ii, iii, ix, 46, 48, 49, 57, 64, 104, 117

Stationary ii, ix, 3, 80, 82, 87-91, 92, 105, 117
Stellium 22, 42, 48, 115
Strength i, ii, iv, vi-xii, 1, 18-20, 22, 23, 30, 32, 41, 44, 45, 47, 64, 65, 81, 82, 87, 89, 90, 91, 95
Structure ii
Succedent ii, 18, 19, 118
Sun i, ii, iii, vi, x, xi, 2, 13, 22, 23, 41, 43, 45, 46, 64, 65, 74, 89, 90, 91, 92-95, 103, 104, 107, 112
Superior conjunction 90
Superior planets vi, 46
Synodic cycle 91-94
Synodic phase ii, 89-91

T

Taurus ii, v, 13, 90
T-cross ii, 45, 46, 48
Terms i, x
Terrestrial state ii, ix, xii, 1, 18-23, 25, 43, 47, 64, 65, 74
Terrestrial strength 18, 41, 44
Trapezoid ii, 47
Trine ii, iii, ix, 46, 47, 49, 57, 64, 111
Triplicity i, 3, 46
Tropical Zodiac v
Trungpa, Chogyam 48
Tyl, Noel 111

U

Unaspected ii, ix, 3, 44, 45, 48, 49, 56-62, 87, 91, 106, 112
Uranus xii, 13, 62, 82, 96, 104

V

Vedic vi, vii, viii, 81-82
Venus i, ii, v, ix-xii, 1, 2, 13, 20, 23, 41, 46, 60, 64, 65, 90-95, 103, 110, 111
Virgo i, 1, 90

W

Waning iii, 47
Water signs i, 49, 119
Waxing iii, 47, 115
Wedge ii, 45, 47
Well-aspected ii, ix, x, xii, 18

Z

Zodiac i, v, x, 1, 56, 80, 95, 97, 111

"Readers have become familiar with [Makransky's] fresh insights into different facets of astrology. In *Thought Forms* he is especially provocative and I strongly recommend its purchase and study." – Ken Gillman, *Considerations*.

"I will fully agree with the statement that 'You've never read a book like this before!" The material is fresh and woven very skillfully to conclusion. I look forward to his next installment of the trilogy." – Marion MacMillan, SHAPE

9780967731537 Buy from Amazon and smashwords.com/b/22859

****

Magical Almanac – http://groups.yahoo.com/group/MagicalAlmanac

is Bob Makransky's free monthly ezine of astrology and magic for thoughtful, intelligent people who are seeking something deeper than the usual New Age astrological fare. *Magical Almanac* usually contains an article on magic, an article on astrology and an almanac of favorable and unfavorable days each month to initiate activities, charge amulets, or cast spells. The *Magical Almanac* files are chock full of great articles on astrology, consciousness, magic for beginners, and Mayan astrology and shamanism.

To subscribe send an e-mail to: MagicalAlmanac-subscribe@yahoogroups.com

Or check it out at: http://groups.yahoo.com/group/MagicalAlmanac

www.DearBrutus.com

is Bob Makransky's personal website offering insightful articles on astrology and magic, as well as Bob's books and astrology services. Also: complete instructions on how to channel spirit guides and how to run past life regressions; free downloadable Mayan Horoscope software; information on the natural treatment of cancer and AIDS; articles on Mayan folklore; humorous short stories, cartoons, and lots, lots more!

Other Books by The Wessex Astrologer

Patterns of the Past
Karmic Connections
Good Vibrations
The Soulmate Myth: A Dream Come
True or Your Worst Nightmare?
The Book of Why
Judy Hall

The Essentials of Vedic Astrology
Lunar Nodes - Crisis and Redemption
Personal Panchanga and the Five
Sources of Light
Komilla Sutton

Astrolocality Astrology
From Here to There
Martin Davis

The Consultation Chart
Introduction to Medical Astrology
Wanda Sellar

The Betz Placidus Table of Houses
Martha Betz

Astrology and Meditation-
The Fearless Contemplation of Change
Greg Bogart

The Book of World Horoscopes
Nicholas Campion

The Moment of Astrology
Geoffrey Cornelius

Life After Grief - An Astrological Guide
to Dealing with Loss
AstroGraphology
Darrelyn Gunzburg

The Houses: Temples of the Sky
Deborah Houlding

Through the Looking Glass
The Magic Thread
Richard Idemon

Temperament: Astrology's
Forgotten Key
Dorian Geiseler Greenbaum

Astrology, A Place in Chaos
Star and Planet Combinations
Bernadette Brady

Astrology and the Causes of War
Jamie Macphail

Flirting with the Zodiac
Kim Farnell

The Gods of Change
Howard Sasportas

Astrological Roots:
The Hellenistic Legacy
Joseph Crane

The Art of Forecasting
using Solar Returns
Anthony Louis

Horary Astrology Re-Examined
Barbara Dunn

Living Lilith - Four Dimensions of the
Cosmic Feminine
M. Kelley Hunter

Your Horoscope in Your Hands
Lorna Green

Primary Directions
Martin Gansten

Classical Medical Astrology
Oscar Hofman

The Door Unlocked:
An Astrological Insight into Initiation
*Dolores Ashcroft Nowicki and Stephanie V.
Norris*

Understanding Karmic Complexes:
Evolutionary Astrology and Regression
Therapy
Patricia L. Walsh

All the Sun Goes Round
Reina James

www.wessexastrologer.com

CPSIA information can be obtained at www.ICGtesting.com
Printed in the USA
BVOW011953070213

312703BV00004B/93/P